Outdoor Insights

STEVE CHAPMAN

HARVEST HOUSE PUBLISHERS
Eugene, OR 97402

Cover by Paz Design Group, Salem, Oregon

Outdoor Insights
Copyright © 1999 by Steve Chapman (text and illustrations)
Published by Harvest House Publishers
Eugene, Oregon 97402

Library of Congress Cataloging-in-Publication Data
Chapman, Steve.
    Outdoor insights / Steve Chapman.
        p.   cm.
    ISBN 0-7369-0059-4
    1. Parent and child.   2. Parent and child—Religious aspects—
Christianity.   3. Family recreation.   4. Outdoor recreation.
I. Title.
HQ755.85.C4913   1999
306.874—dc21   98-45820
                                                                              CIP

99 00 01 02 03 04 / BP / 10 9 8 7 6 5 4 3 2 1

A special thanks to my children, Nathan and Heidi, for going outside with me. To Annie for letting us go. And . . . to God for His wonderful creation.

Contents

1

Beyond the Squeaky Door

My deep love for being in the great outdoors has caused me to do some strange things. I've been guilty, for example, of staring trance-like out the windows of airport lobbies, nearly missing the call to board a flight because somewhere out there, beyond the runway, in a field, there had to be a hawk swooping down to capture its prey from the grass, and I couldn't help but watch. I can also get lost in a beautiful, towering mountain in the distance where I imagine I am hiking or hunting . . . or both.

I confess, I am easily dazed by the sight of the outdoors, especially when I know I can't be out there! I recall one instance when I was so distracted I had to force myself to "wake up" and remember what I was doing. Annie and I were performing a concert in a church in Pennsylvania, one of the prettiest states in America. We had walked to the stage and positioned ourselves at the microphones and had begun to sing the first song. I scanned the congregation as I usually do to get a feel for the make-up of the audience. I looked to my far right, and was stunned! I saw something I had not noticed when we arrived for set-up that afternoon. Just over the heads of those sitting in that section was a large window reaching from the ceiling nearly to the floor. It was 7 P.M. and still daylight, and the scene through that window took my breath away. . . . It would have rendered any whitetail deer hunter (which I certainly am) insensible. Now, there were no bucks or does out there. It was just a field, edged with one of the most beautiful tree lines imaginable. Right behind it was a hillside that had a forest of unusually big trees, the type you long to find where you can set up a treestand over the trails that lead the deer to their feeding areas.

I just knew that any minute, a huge Pennsylvania monster buck was going to step out on the edge of that field and graze in the evening sun. And I didn't want to miss him. I was as sure of it as I was of playing a "G" chord on the song we were singing. I thought of every excuse I could to look in that direction as often as possible. However, I knew singing exclusively to that portion of the crowd would look awkward. So . . . I forced myself to reduce the frequency of turning toward the window. I also found the perfect way to scout out that field.

On stage, Annie normally stands on my right for two reasons. One, so the neck of the guitar won't hit her on the jaw or hide her lovely face. And two, the sound hole of my instrument points in her direction and that makes it easier for her to follow my playing. It appeared that I was looking her way, but in reality, I looked just to the left of her right cheek and could see the meadow that was calling my name. I gazed out that window regularly. The audience must have thought, "What a loving husband!"

Then it happened. Annie stepped back from the microphone after the song ended and suddenly . . . dead silence. It had come my turn to speak but I was in "hunt" mode and missed the cue. I stood there still gawking out the window.

Annie cleared her throat in that "special" way a wife does when she needs to get her husband's attention. Shocked back into reality, embarrassment caused me to stutter as I stumbled into the introduction of our next song. Unfortunately, the hunt was over. It was back to the business at hand for me.

I'll never forget how I had to struggle to concentrate on the music. Also, I'll never forget what a miserable failure I felt like after that concert. I determined that the next time I faced an inviting window like the one in that church, I would make sure our set-up faced the baptismal pool. I am happy to report I never went through that kind of battle again . . . primarily because we've never been in another church with a window view like that one in Pennsylvania!

I am fully convinced that this wonderful preoccupation I have for God's great outdoors began when I was a youngster in a little town in West Virginia. And I lay all the precious blame on my mother. This was her "doing"—and I love her for it. How many times did she say, "GO OUTSIDE AND PLAY!"? Those words reverberate in my heart even today. Little did she know she was guiding me to the very therapy a grown man needs to endure adulthood. She had no idea that every time she sent me outside, she was spooning medicine into my soul.

And so . . . I did go outside. And I played with a passion! It was the easiest obedience I can remember. There was something mystical about pushing open that old, creaking screen door and stepping out into the big world. When I let the door go, the force of the long spring, stretched to its maximum, sent that pine-wood frame flying back to the door jam. I can still hear it slam behind me. That noise woke me from the stupor I felt from being inside so long. (By the way, though the slam of that door nearly drove my mother insane, she rarely complained. Well . . . maybe a time or two. But now I believe that she endured the jarring of the walls because she knew that she could enjoy some much-needed solitude.)

As I stood on the porch, pulled my little britches up, and licked my lips, I remember looking left and right, all wide-eyed and full of anticipation. In the vast expanse of my universe waited a myriad of opportunities for a kid.

First, I checked to see if any other friends had been "released" as well. If not, I quickly "wandered" over to their house and asked the question that has led many a young boy to either destructive or constructive mischief: "Can Bobby come out and play?"

Sometimes the answer was a quick and resounding, "NO!" I didn't need to ask why. My friend's confinement was usually the punishment for a previous misuse of our freedom. It was the most dreaded of all sentences and could not have been worse for us little guys.

Many times, however, my request for companionship was greeted with words that make a young boy's heart jump. "Sure, he'll be right out!" Another door would squeak and slam, and our quest for adventure would begin! It usually started with one of the most dangerous questions one boy can ask another. "Watch-ya wanna do?"

Could it be that, upon hearing those words fall from the mouth of a little boy, heaven braces itself? Might it be that God summons extra angels of protection at that moment and sends them earthward? Yet, even with the risks involved, He allows the adventurers to go on. I believe He does because He knows what life-changing insights await a child who spends time in His great outdoors. For example, a child that digs in the dirt might someday grasp the incredible fact that it was from dust that we came. Those young eyes can be the window to the soul. And in the night, in a makeshift, backyard campsite, they might look with amazement at the innumerable stars that hang above them, and better view the awesomeness of their Creator. And someday, when someone tells them they need to build their spiritual house on the sure foundation of Christ, they'll remember the solid rocks their young feet once played on. As a result, that eternal truth will be understood more easily.

Perhaps God is pleased when the ears of a child enjoy the music that the springtime frogs make, or the songs the birds sing. When a kid stops to listen to the symphony of the sounds made by things like bugs and dogs, thunder and waterfalls, could it be that God knows the child will eventually want to thank someone for it all? And He'll gladly wait for their gratitude. Therefore, God welcomes a young one into His great outdoors.

Now in mid-life (assuming I'll reach my nineties!), I am many miles and many years away from childhood. However, I have not at all said good-bye to the passion I hold in my heart for the sound of that squeaky door announcing, "You're free!!" I will be forever grateful that my mother insisted I "go outside and play!" Her words have echoed in my soul for all these years, and now . . . they have made their way to my children.

Annie and I have two wonderful kids—Nathan and Heidi. They have not only heard me say the words of my mother, but they often hear a slight twist in the statement. I love to say it this way, "*Let's* go outside and play!" And here's the scary part. Annie has heard me, the biggest kid in the family, ask my children that dangerous question. "Watcha wanna do?!" Yet, she sighs and resolves to the impending adventure because she wants what I want. Knowing that God can be seen in His great outdoors, we want our kids to find Him and know Him.

I'm not sure if any of us will ever fully understand God in this life. If we did, perhaps we wouldn't need Him. However, I'm sure we can learn more about His ways and His character while out in His creation. This book is about the way I've used some of the outdoor activities we've enjoyed together to help our children grow in character. Because I still love to go outside and play, I'm grateful that some of life's best lessons can be learned . . . beyond the squeaky door!

2

And the Long Journey Begins

I finally figured out why Nathan and I like the game of golf as much as we enjoy deer hunting. It's because both involve going to the woods and looking for something! However, as great as a day of pursuing the whitetail can be, there is one thing about a walk on the fairways that can be better than hunting. When we get home after a round of golf . . . *we don't have to clean it!*

Someone once referred to a day on the golf course as "a good walk ruined." Any of us who use our irons to dig divots the depth of industrial drainage ditches can appreciate that description. Yet, the challenge of the game seems to call us back to itself . . . and amazingly enough, we return. Nathan and I notice that it's usually on the very last hole of the round that the course makes its move, enticing us to come back. After dribbling the ball around the fairways and writing on our score card numbers that rival the national debt, lo and behold, we par the 18th. We go to the clubhouse with spirits raised and sure that if we try just one more time tomorrow, everything about our swing will fall into place and the course will be conquered. Somehow we leave the last green confident that our next stop is the PGA Tour. Of course, that dream is shattered on the first tee the next time out.

For those who cannot appreciate the game and jokingly refer to it as "barnyard pool," I encourage you to first go to a local driving range and try your hand at hitting a golf ball. Then, after you've beaned a few innocent onlookers in the parking lot and realize it's not as easy as it looks, I recommend you go to a professional tournament for a day of watching the experts. Consistently hitting a little ball with any accuracy at all requires an enormous amount of talent and concentration.

The first tournament Nathan and I went to was in Memphis, Tennessee. It was the St. Jude/Federal Express Classic. We endured the intense August heat and watched some of the game's greats. We were amazed at how little they seemed to notice the crowds of people lining the greens and fairways. Their eyes were fixed solidly on the ball and their next shot. As they walked by us, sometimes within a club length, their expressions nearly shocked us. Most of them appeared to be in a trance. With hardly any prompting, everyone in the gallery united in minimizing the distractions, especially when the flag came out of the hole. The player stood over his ball on the putting surface, and the quiet that engulfed the green seemed sacred. The emotion could be cut with a knife. Some of the family members of the pros were present and although the players surely loved them deeply, Nathan and I noted that they too seemed to be ignored by golfing husbands, dads, and sons who passed them by. The competition did strange things to their minds. That day our appreciation level for the talents of the pros, and their families, grew to mountainous heights. It's a tough way to make a living . . . but they love it!

One of the products of that tournament was an intense desire in our hearts to hurry home and on to the course. That's a phenomenon (actually an affliction) that boys of all ages deal with, and it starts young. If you don't believe it, next time you go to a high school football game, look along the sidelines outside the fence. There'll be a parallel game going on, played with a ball made with used duct tape. The players are all the little guys who were so inspired by the sight on the field that they mysteriously and uncontrollably left the bleachers and congregated off to the side to get their "fix." Nathan and I were "itching" to play so we set off to our local nine-hole, three-par course to do some scratching.

We invited one of Nathan's little friends to go along. Young Jason had never played golf or even held a club in his hands. We were a little more experienced and for some reason, perhaps a subliminal need for taking along our own gallery, we overlooked the encumbrance that our third participant would be. Our visions of golf grandeur were wiped away on the first tee, however, when Jason took his first swing. Nathan had hit a decent drive about 75 yards toward the green that waited 90 yards away. I bounced off behind the green and only had a chip shot to get back to the "dance floor." Jason, on the other hand, was trying desperately to just connect. The wind off his club felt good in the August heat, but Nathan and I looked at each other and just shook our heads. Finally, the little human helicopter made contact with his ball and it popped out of the tee box and landed ten yards away in the deep rough. As the three of us picked up our clubs, Jason ran toward his shot in excitement. He actually was enjoying the experience. I looked at my exasperated son and said, ". . . And the long journey begins!"

Nathan and I had a great first hole. We still wonder if the slower pace of play helped us, but I collected a bogey. Nathan had a double, which was very good for a ten-year-old. However, it was downhill from the second hole on. The "judge not, lest ye be judged" lesson became painfully applicable for Nathan and me. We started hitting shots that made Jason look pretty good. We ended up waving several groups on through while the three of us looked under rocks and in heavy brush for our limited supply of balls. When we finally finished, our scorecard showed that we had managed to get our money's worth. We calculated that at $4.00 for nine holes, it cost us about a penny a shot. Pretty cheap fun, eh?

We headed home, dropped a very tired Jason off at his house, and then Nathan and I talked about our game. We eventually laughed about it, but I also took it as an opportunity to relay an important message. "Son, I don't know about you, but I was embarrassed out there today. Some of the people we held up seemed rather upset, and rightly so. As much as I'd like to skip the lessons and go straight to the leader board, it's not gonna happen. Not with this game . . . or any other. The truth is, the golf course is not the place to learn to play. This sport is best learned at the practice range, and I suggest finding an instructor."

That summer, we invested in a four-week golf school at a nearby course. To save money, I sent Nathan and he passed on his "learnings" to me. We were convinced we did the right thing.

The lesson I tried to convey to my son that day became vividly clear not too long afterward. He discovered a real interest in playing the guitar, and began working on it seriously. His desire to perform with us on stage grew very quickly, and right away we could tell that he felt he was ready. He dropped a number of hints that he was waiting for our cue. Parentally, we were tempted to let him try. Professionally, however, we knew he wasn't ready. We decided in this case to forego the good character that failure can build and spare him the discouragement that might permanently damage his interest in music. While we waited for the right moment, I detected his discouragement about the delay. So I reminded him of the "journey with Jason" around the golf course. Because we believe the lyrics in our songs carry an important message, we are concerned about the way they reach the ears. During a concert we get only one performance of each song, and like the golf shot, we have to try to not go "out of bounds" with errant shots. Every swing of the club, or in our case, pluck of the string, is precious. I said, "Son, to play guitar on stage before you're ready would be like learning to play golf during the Masters in Augusta."

Nathan graciously accepted the instruction and continued to work on his instrument.

Today, at 21, Nathan is one of the finest guitarists I know. His well-developed skill has yielded some impressive results. When he was 17 he did his first studio recording and later that year he directed a full band as they recorded a fifty-minute, live concert video. During the filming, he was joined on stage by a guitarist whom he deeply admires and aspires to emulate, that being Mr. Phil Keaggy. At that moment, Nathan was, so to speak, "with the big guys at Augusta."

Since that memorable evening, our son has gone on to produce and perform on two duet albums with his sister Heidi, as well as producing and playing guitar on five albums by Annie and me. We fully trust him and the talent he has wisely cultivated. Interestingly enough, however, his game of golf has suffered. We're both still bogey and double-bogey golfers. I suppose you could say we have chosen to fail at that game, because there are so many other things at which we want to succeed.

3

I Have Scars to Prove It

Heidi also gained an important insight from the game of golf. In her case, we never made it to the local course at all. She found her first birdie in our front yard. I'll never forget it.

I had about three minutes of free time one day and needed a break from my work. So I went to the garage, got my clubs, and went to hit some chip shots around the front yard. Heidi came out of the house and saw me "playing" and asked if she could join in the fun. She was about eight at the time and I couldn't refuse her charming request. I handed her a five iron out of my bag, showed her how to "choke up" on the shaft, and she proceeded to step back and took a swing. I was pleasantly surprised. She had a very natural flow with the club and my first thought when I saw her fluid swing was, "SCHOLARSHIPS!" I immediately concluded, "She can use these 'sticks' to save us some 'green' when it comes time for her post-high-school education!"

I praised her for her form and said, "Heidi, let me show you a couple of things about the golf swing that might help." I turned her around with her back to me, put my hand on top of her curly of hair, and nudged her head downward. Then I showed her a small clump of grass near her feet in the middle of her stance and said, "Pretend that grass is the ball. Keep your eyes on it all the way through the swing. Now . . . rock your club back and forth and try to make the head of the club take the same path over the grass each time."

She slightly misunderstood my directions and what happened next is blurred, but here's what I remember: Heidi assumed I meant for her to take a full swing, and when she did, she suddenly realized her dad was standing behind her and she tried to stop the heavy club. It whipped in her hands and the front edge of the five-iron blade caught me squarely on my left cheekbone. I grabbed my face, wheeled around, and staggered across the yard, seeing and hearing and feeling my daughter's first birdie!

Heidi took off running. She probably thought, "I have one club. Dad's got a whole bag full of them. I'm outta here!" She ran up onto the porch and turned around to look my way, perhaps to see if I were dead. I saw her looking at me with an expression of grief and horror and I yelled, "It's O.K., sweetheart, it doesn't hurt!" And it really didn't. No one feels pain when they're completely numb!

I continued to press my fingers onto the bump that was growing underneath, and I stood there waiting for Heidi to walk back over to me so I could offer her some reassurance that I was O.K. I decided to try to console her in her regrets and I removed my fingers from my cheek. I said, "Look, sweetie, its only a bump." But I saw blood spurt out of my face like the stream from a water fountain when you push the button.

Heidi saw it too. She let go a frightened scream and ran into the house. I grew a little weak at the sight and wondered how serious the wound really was. I was a little perturbed, too, that my daughter left me to expire in the front yard. I didn't realize she had gone for help. Suddenly, Annie came running out of the house with a clean towel.

She immediately determined, "emergency room." I balked at the idea, like big babies usually do, but she kept it up. She used a line on me I had heard before when other parts of my body had needed medical attention: "That cheek may be on your face, but it's mine. I'm taking my cheek to the hospital. You can come with me if you want to!" I knew I had to surrender. That's a battle no man should ever try to win. Besides, a dish towel soaked with my own blood made me believe she was right . . . again.

It took eight stitches, four inside and four outside, to close the wound. When we returned home, the kids met us in the driveway. As I removed the bandage to show everyone the sewing job, Nathan gasped at the sight. When Annie saw the shape of the cut she said, "Well . . . looks like your golf game has a slice in it!" Heidi quietly grimaced and said nothing.

Later that evening I noticed Heidi kept her distance from me. I knew she was hurting, feeling terrible about the incident. As we sat in our den, I called her over to me and pulled her up onto my lap. I embraced her and said, "Heidi, I am so grateful for the scar I'm gonna have on my cheek."

"Really, dad?"

"That's right, sweetheart, because from now on I'll be able to tell folks that I love my children and that I spend time with my kids. . . . and I have scars to prove it!"

I thought I saw the glimmer of a smile on her face. Then a thought came to me that I know was from Heaven. My heart pounded with excitement as I said to my daughter,

". . . And Heidi, there's someone else who loves you even more than I do. . . . and He has scars to prove it!" Then we talked about the sacrifice Jesus Christ made for all of us and about the marks of His boundless love in His hands and feet.

Even now, when I look in the mirror and see that "slice" on my face, I remember that afternoon and the deeper bond my daughter and I have as a result of being outdoors together that day.

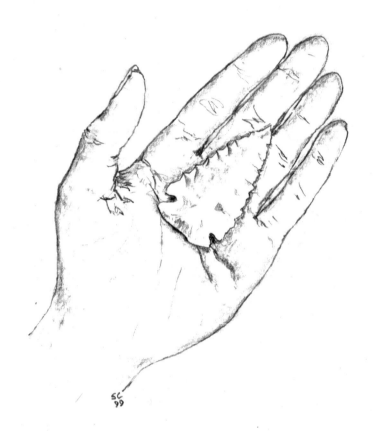

4

Treasures of Truth

An unknown man crouched behind a large, moss-covered rock and cautiously watched the approaching whitetail deer. Its ivory-colored antlers glistened in the early morning sun! The hunter's heart pounded with excitement as he pressed his fingers onto the string of his hand-made bow. The man's dark eyes focused firmly on the target, a tuft of raised hair over the deer's lung area, and he slowly and methodically came to full draw.

Suddenly, the quiet snap of the string sent the arrow streaking toward fur and flesh. Much to the hunter's surprise, however, at the sound of the string the body of the big deer instantly dropped in preparation to bound away from danger, and the wooden missile sailed just over his back, burying itself deeply in the soft, leafy floor of the forest. With the animal out of sight, the man accepted his failure. But before continuing on to another patch of woods to search for needed food, he quickly tried to find the arrow that was tipped with his masterpiece of stone. The thick bed of leaves and brush had swallowed it and his search yielded only a loss of valuable time. So he moved on.

Behind him, in its grave of rich, dark dirt, the work of his skilled hands, remained. The wood, leather, pine tar, turkey feather, and the hunter himself returned to dust. Then, one summer day . . . 140 years later, something wonderful happened. A brown-eyed, curly haired girl looked down on the soft, dried dirt of the freshly plowed cornfield. In wide-eyed fascination, she saw the only surviving evidence that the great hunter had ever existed. With fingers trembling, she carefully pinched the exposed tip of the triangle-shaped stone and rescued it. She jumped straight up and yelled, "Dad, I found one!"

That young girl was my daughter Heidi. The story of how the arrowhead ended up at her feet is, as you probably guessed, a product of my imagination, but the treasure she found is very real. That priceless relic is now among some other collectibles we cherish. To say the least, arrowhead hunting is one of our most favorite things to do. Fortunately, we live in an area where Native Americans had settled many years before, and the opportunity to search for signs of their lives is precious to us.

There is something unique about digging and exploring the farmlands around our home, searching for remnants of those who once dwelt here. A strangely indescribable emotion accompanies every find, without exception, even if it's simply a broken piece of an arrowhead.

Our usual ritual is, once the treasure is found and carefully removed from the dirt, we lay it in the palm of one hand and gingerly wipe away the excess mud. Then we wrap our fingers around it and clutch it to our hearts. For a moment, as we stand quietly at the spot where it was found, we first take in the joy of knowing that by holding the arrowhead, the hands of the present are touching the hands of the past. Then we close our eyes and wonder what the person who made the article was like. What did he look like? What about his family? Of course we never get a clear view of the archer—he is lost in the distant mist of time. But the fact that he once walked on this very ground always amazes us.

The excitement and mystique of uncovering a piece of history that awaits us in the soil of Tennessee keeps us going back whenever we can. Anxious anticipation always fills our hearts when we plan to head for the fields and stream beds. And, surprisingly, nearly each time we go we return to our home with a find. The field has probably been searched many times over in decades past, but it still seems to hold undiscovered artifacts. More than once we have climbed into the truck after a time of hunting arrowheads and one of us has said, "I wonder how many we walked over today?" And it is in the "finding and re-finding" that an important insight could be passed on to Heidi.

In the rich soil of God's Word treasures of truth wait to be revealed to us as a result of diligent searching. And it seems that no matter how many times we walk through a passage, we discover something new and wonderful.

One example of this is Psalm 119:105: *"Thy word is lamp to my feet, a light to my path."* On first reading, one can rejoice in knowing that God's Word is there to give light and guidance to our journey through time. What a blessing and comfort He has provided.

But . . . when the words are read again, an additional revelation comes to us. Notice that the light is given only to the feet and not to the distant road ahead. We can assume that in God's great mercy, He gives us the grand opportunity to trust Him for the steps on the path beyond the light and unseen by our fleshly eyes. Thus, we recognize that putting our faith and trust in Him is our only hope of ever getting to our destination safely. (One verse, two truths. And I'm confident there are more!)

In the same way that Heidi and I have trained our eyes to inspect every inch of ground for an arrowhead, so can we carefully read the Scriptures. In the fields, we have learned not to ignore even a tiny chip of flint that protrudes from a mound of dirt. I especially remember one small point I saw that was hardly the size of the tip of a scissors blade. I reached down and pinched it with my fingers and pulled. Lo and behold, it was attached to a long, slender, beautifully shaped spear head.

Through that experience, I was able to show Heidi that we must look very carefully at the pages of the Scriptures, keeping in mind that the words on the paper are like the top soil in the fields. Wonderful treasures can be found not only on the surface, but below it as well. The key is to return to it as often as possible, turning it over and over in our minds and hearts by meditating on it.

In our curio cabinets and in a shadow box in our home, you'll find the arrowheads we've been honored to pluck from the grasp of their muddy old graves. Instead of them remaining a silent testimony to their makers, these relics of stone now proudly announce to those whose eyes fall on them that once their creator lived, worked, hunted, fathered children, dreamed, fought, and subdued the earth. And long after our house has fallen prey to the ravages of time and is bulldozed back into the ground, and well after our bodies return to the dust from which they came, those stony works of the unknown craftsmen will remain in the rubble to be rescued by someone else in the far distant future.

We hold on to them because each time we see them they remind us of some important facts. First, they tell us of the past and the peoples they represent. Second, those pieces of artfully shaped flint remind Heidi and me of some wonderful times we have had together in the great outdoors. Finally, and most wonderfully, those stone arrowheads will help us remember that there are treasures of truth in the Word of God that wait to be uncovered. And unlike the stone that will eventually deteriorate into unrecognizable particles of dust, His Word *"will stand forever"* (Isaiah 40:8).

5

Camping Is . . .

When we were kids, my sister and I would take a blanket to the kitchen, drape it over a couple of dining room chairs, pull the corners tight and hold them to the linoleum with the legs of the big table. Suddenly, we had a tent. We'd crawl in, giggling, and hide inside our cloth fortress. The interesting thing was, in the confinement of that small space, I felt a wonderful freedom. Perhaps it was the relief of being out of a parent's eyesight for a moment. Or, maybe, having walls of my own choosing made me sense a degree of my own free will. Whatever the reason, our tent was a symbol of liberty. And to this day, whenever those new-fangled fiberglass tent poles come out of their bag and snap together in my hands, I feel an impending freedom. It's been with me through all these years.

Then one day, many years later, something startling happened. Nathan and Heidi, very young at the time, dragged one of Annie's homemade bedspreads to our dining room and made their own "quilted cathedral of freedom."

I'm not certain I ever instructed them in the art of indoor camping. They probably had seen a picture of a campsite or an actual tent in their travels with us. I don't know. But without any prompting from me, they were *kitchen camping*.

Then the thought occurred to me, *Maybe they are responding to some instinct that is born in every human being.* It seems that the urge to wander off into a wilderness and find one's own place to dwell is innate and undeniable. Perhaps my kids were showing their own initial signs of a desire for independence. After all, look what happened to me several years after my first kitchen campsite. Here I am, living 425 miles from my parents' house, totally on my own.

So . . . if your little kids haven't yet dropped a blanket over a piece of furniture and made a tent, brace yourself . . . they will. And when they do, keep in mind that they're on their way out of your lives! It's just a matter of time.

For that reason, I decided to crawl inside the tent with Nathan and Heidi instead of just standing by and letting them quietly disappear over the hill of time. I wanted to show them that looking through a zip-open door can give us one of the most valuable views of life a person can have. I wanted them to know that camping is so much more than bugs, blisters, and bumpy beds. For example, camping is an opportunity to learn an important lesson about . . . CONTENTMENT.

Our perceptive friend, Mike Hudson, came back to town one Monday after a camping trip and noted how many times he had heard himself say the phrase, "I can't wait to . . ." He said his weekend sounded something like this: As they loaded the car with their equipment he said, "I can't wait to get to the mountains!" Once they were near their destination . . . "I can't wait till camp is set up!" While they were pounding the stakes into the ground to anchor the tent . . . "I can't wait till the fire is roaring!" On and on it went. While he was doing one thing, his thoughts were ahead on the next chore to the point that he couldn't enjoy what he was presently doing. "I can't wait till the food is ready . . . Can't wait till the dishes are done . . . Can't wait till we get in our sleeping bags," and, "I just can't wait till morning gets here!" Before the weekend was over, though, Mike had come to his senses and realized that all the joy of the experience was getting lost in his current attitude of discontentment.

Drawing from Mike's valuable well of wisdom, whenever I went camping with Nathan and Heidi after that, I determined not to let our trip be a frustrating exercise in anxiety. Instead, I consciously slowed down, relaxed, and purposefully tried to teach them to cherish all the steps of the journey as we took them, and not just the last one.

Camping is also . . . COOPERATION.

There's a story about a family who drove into a state park after a long journey. They were assigned a site at the registration building, and when they pulled into "their" spot, it was still daylight. When the dad put the car in park and set the emergency brake, the back doors suddenly flew open and his two kids quickly jumped out and ran to the tailgate. Tarps, tents, anchor stakes, and lawn chairs sailed out onto the ground and within minutes, with the kids' help, their campsite reached full readiness.

Next to them was another family who had arrived earlier that day. The father watched as the young newcomers worked feverishly to complete their task. Quite impressed, he wandered over and approached the other dad. "I couldn't help but notice how incredibly industrious your children are. How did you instill that kind of work ethic in them?" he asked.

The humbled father admitted, "Well, sir . . . thank you for your compliment, but you see, we have a system. No one goes to the bathroom till camp is set up!"

This dad undoubtedly had learned that getting cooperation from his kids took some creativity. Previous experiences must have shown him the excitement children feel when they are about to enter the merriment of spending "a night in the great outdoors." The anticipation can be so great that they focus only on the fun.

However, this dad overcame a temptation that most fathers face when we take our families camping. We want to do all the work of setting up and maintaining a campsite. We know it is a ton of effort, but we think that if we do it ourselves, it's done more quickly and often more efficiently! And we think it frees our kids to "have more fun!" Yet this dad knew that that approach not only would leave him very tired and grumpy, it would also lead his children to believe that their help was not important. Because he cared enough to get them involved, he passed on to his kids one of the best lessons that camping has to offer—the gratification of cooperation.

I encourage you to let your kids pitch the tent even though it may be noticeably crooked when it's erected. Or let them boil the beans and don't worry about the black sludge they leave on the bottom of the pot the first time or two. (With a good knife, it'll scrape off. Plus it can taste pretty good when you're near starvation!) And show them how to start a safe fire without destroying half of the state's timberland. There are a lot of other duties for which you can enlist their help. In the long run, if we don't allow them the opportunity to help out now, how will they be able to pass along the art of camping to those who will come after us?

And camping is . . . CRISIS.

When a family returns from a camping excursion, ask them, "Did you have a good time?" If they shrug their shoulders with a casual, "Yeah. It was fine," you can rest assured the trip was uneventful and left few moments to recall.

However, if you ask them that question and they respond with, "OH, MAN! IT WAS GREAT! You wouldn't believe what a weekend we had!" What would that tell you? I guarantee you they experienced at least one crisis, and possibly more. For some reason, the low points during the trip become the high points afterward. It's the black bear outside the tent, foraging the backpacks, that causes us to hug one another. It's the slip of the foot, the slide down a bank into a cold river, a fire to dry the clothes, and talk of the close call that sticks in our minds. The crisis becomes the point at which we bond.

When Heidi and I talk about our first trip to the Appalachian Trail, our minds immediately go to two unforgettable moments along the way. One was the unending climb up Whitetop Mountain. We started in very nice weather and then it turned cold and nasty. The wind caused the dense fog to soak into our clothes clear to the skin and we thought we would freeze to death. We started looking for a place to hunker down for the night, and finally about dark, we came to a stand of heavy cedars. We hurriedly set up our tent under a leaning tree before noticing that the tree was actually cracked.

Then the second crisis began. Too tired to force ourselves to move our site, we crawled inside our two-man tent and tried to rest. Our bags were warm and dry, but we didn't sleep a wink the entire night. The large, broken cedar above us swayed and creaked in the wind, and we were kept awake by the fear of being crushed.

As the sun began to rise, we crawled out of our tattered tent and were delighted to find that the storm had passed and we had survived. Somehow, tired as we were, exhilaration strengthened our steps down the other side of Whitetop. We had come through the ordeal together!

What reason is there to hug and rejoice when an experience is bland? When they ask you, "Did you have a good time?" a survivable crisis or two always puts an explanation point at the end of your "YES!" (May all your dilemmas be safe ones!)

Camping is . . . CONNECTING.

Somewhere in the back of our modern minds there is a question we'd like to ask, but we're afraid to know the answer: "Could we make it through the wilderness like our ancestors did?" If all our conveniences, such as water at the tap, inside toilets, electricity, and forced air, were suddenly stripped away from us, would we be strong enough to carry on? Camping with children presents a grand opportunity to give them a small taste of the stamina required of the pioneers, like Lewis and Clark, as they passed through the rugged, unexplored territory of North America. Of course, with our soft, self-inflating air mattress under us, the high-tech, wind- and rain-proof tent over our heads, and our pre-packaged, freeze-dried meals, it's tough to fully understand those early pioneers' unbelievable courage. Still, it's a chance to connect with the brave folks who managed with not much more than a sleeping roll and the flicker of a flame. I noticed that when Nathan and Heidi returned from "roughing it" in the wild to a warm bedroom and an adjustable shower, their level of gratitude for our way of life was always up. That connection is worth the trouble in many a dad's estimation.

Camping is . . . CONVERSATION.

With the absence of electricity, which means no TV or sound systems when we're camping, we have few options for entertainment. About all that's left is . . . talk.

For some dads, the thought of conversing with a kid is traumatic. At a campsite, as the orange colors of the fire-light dance on the faces of a dad and a child, when the deafening sound of silence fills the air, it might be excruciating for the father when nothing is said. How welcome is the sound of the crackle that the fire brings to the quietness.

So . . . what do we do to solve the dialogue dilemma? Here are some ideas. We can start with "chit-chat!" In our family, we like to recall favorite movie lines like, "Does your dog bite?" from the *Pink Panther* series. Another all time favorite is from *What About Bob.* "Baby steps to 4 o'clock!" These quips can jump-start a conversation any day.

Ask some questions like, "What was the happiest day of your life?" Or, "What was the saddest day?" Another idea is to tell the son or daughter about the day they were born. What was happening in the hospital, in the family, or in the nation at that time in history.

Go to the past and work your way forward. Soon, you'll discover that both of you are swimming in the refreshing pool of information that is stored in your minds and hearts.

You never know, the conversation might lead to words like, "I love you!"

Finally, camping can be . . . CHURCH.

When your sabbath comes and finds you crawling out of a tent instead of crawling into a pew, church can, and should, still happen. And of course, what a wonderful cathedral the sky becomes under the Creator's mighty canopy, a view not obstructed by walls! A song, a scripture and commentary, some prayer time for loved ones who are probably worried sick about you, and even communion if you plan ahead, would be a wonderful way to start the day.

With simplicity being one of the abiding themes of the camping experience, a worship service while sitting on a log around a breakfast fire can be very uplifting spiritually. It is a great setting to remind a child of the *"simplicity . . . of devotion to Christ"* that we should desire as found in 2 Corinthians 11:3. And with the campsite as a backdrop, you could use the following camping analogy to teach your kids about the only One who is able to bind all believers together. This story comes from the heart of our friend, Bob Hughey.

A long time ago, Christ Jesus began a journey through the earth. With Him were all of His followers. They walked with Him from sunrise to sunset that first day, and then it came time to rest. Jesus built a campfire and His followers pitched their tents. Prior to retiring for the night, Jesus taught His people. That evening He instructed them about the importance of baptism and the joy of following Him in that act of obedience. Jesus and many of His followers went on to bed. However, some of them stayed up, sitting around the campfire and discussing the Master's teaching on baptism until late in the night. Finally, they too went to sleep.

Jesus arose the next morning and continued on with those who had rested with Him. However, those who had stayed up late, also slept late and when they woke up to find the others had moved on, they decided to stay where Jesus had taught so eloquently on baptism.

The next night, something similar happened after Jesus taught the others about the importance of the communion of the saints. He shared bread and wine with His people, they partook, then retired with their Lord. However, some stayed up and discussed the beauty of the communion experience. The next morning, those late-night folks, not fully rested when Jesus traveled on with the others, stayed behind at that site.

Night after night, Jesus delivered His life changing truths around glowing campfires. And night after night portions of His followers talked far into the morning and missed their Master's departure.

This took place until one day, Jesus turned around and there was no one behind Him. He looked back through time and saw all those who had once been so close were now fragmented, huddled tightly around the various campfires of truth. His heart broke.

Today, in His great compassion and love for His followers, He is walking back through those camps where shrines have mistakenly been erected to worship only a single part of His glorious truth. And with open arms He is bidding them, "Follow Me. Come and follow Me!"

Though only an analogy, this story has a powerful ring and describes the times so well. Using the environment of a campsite, I have shared it with Heidi and Nathan. I believe it has helped them understand that when it comes to following Christ, camping can be dangerous if we don't pick up and move on when He leads.

6

The Homecoming

When I look back through the years at the lifestyle Annie and I required of our children, I can't help but wonder what long-term effect it will have on their lives. Nathan and Heidi spent most of their childhood, as well as their teen years, strapped in a seat of a van, a rental car, or an airplane. Their days were filled with hours and hours of confinement in a waiting room that moved. Then, as if that weren't enough, when they arrived at our destination, they had to pile into a hotel room and get ready for a concert where, for the rest of the evening, they were on stage.

Do I feel guilty for what we put them through? In one way, yes. Our work cost them dearly in some areas where most kids don't have to sacrifice. For example, they were never able to be involved in a team sport such as football, soccer, etc. Most games fell on the weekend and when Fridays and Saturdays came, we were off and running to another town to sing. Add to that the other activities their friends shared while Nathan and Heidi were away. I admit that sometimes I regret having "inflicted" my kids with the calling I felt to a mission in music.

Knowing that our children were car-bound, airplane-bound, hotel- and concert-hall-bound most weekends, I tried to be careful to give them a break from the routine as often as I could. One of the best ways was to stop the van, get outside, and do something different! (Of course, stopping the airliner took some doing!) When they were very small and nothing else was available, we could always seem to find a McDonald's Playground. As they got older, it took a little more creativity and advance planning, and we were able to do a variety of things. We went through a potato chip factory in Indiana and rode horses in Montana. (By the way, Heidi's horse was named "Lady." When we started up the mountain, I was behind her on my horse. The strain that her animal experienced revealed that Lady was not very lady-like. Whew! She must've gotten into the cabbage patch!)

Many times, the opportunities to run free in the great outdoors came as a pleasant surprise. Without knowing beforehand, it was always a joy to see the kids' faces when a chance for adventure came up. We have been with folks who had access to swimming pools, snow-ski slopes, water-ski boats, 4-wheelers, a hot air balloon, small airplanes and motorcycles. Unless I detected danger, or the person offering seemed irresponsible, I usually agreed to their taking part because I knew the kids needed to expend some energy.

One unexpected outing took place in Norfolk, Virginia. We were in concert there on a Friday evening and the next day we were to be in Winston-Salem, North Carolina. As we waited in the airplane for our departure, a flight attendant came to our row and handed me a note. It read, "Call the pastor in Winston-Salem!" I hurriedly exited the plane and called the number. I returned to my family and asked them to quickly gather their things and follow me. When they asked why, I told them, "The church had a serious fire last night and our concert there is canceled. We'll stay here until Sunday."

What would we do with an unplanned 24-hour stay in Norfolk without a concert?

First we checked into a hotel around 10 A.M. As we unpacked, an idea came to me that I decided to present to my family. "Annie, how would you like to be alone in the room for a few hours while the kids and I go somewhere?" (A husband should never ask his wife that question in the presence of the children. It leaves her with the awkward challenge of how to answer an excited "Yes!" without making the kids think she never wants to see them again. *Of course* she would cherish a few hours of solitude!) Annie answered with remarkable wisdom, "Well dear, if you're sure it's O.K. with you, and the kids can get along without me for a while, I suppose I'll be fine here." Under her breath she said, "Don't throw me in that briar patch!"

Then the kids began, "Where are we going, Daddy? What are we going to do?"

I answered with a tone of anticipation, "This city and the neighboring cities of Portsmouth and Virginia Beach are Naval Stations. Some big ships have docked near here and I want to go see one of them. Virginia Beach is the air station where I spent nearly two years of my life. They told me at the hotel desk that an aircraft carrier, The USS SARATOGA-CVA 60, is sitting at the dock. That's the sister ship to the one I was on, The USS FORRESTAL-CVA 59, which is now decommissioned." (That made me feel old!)

The kids' eyes grew wide with excitement and they cried out, "Whoa! You're kidding! Right?"

I said, "Nope, let's go!"

We boarded a city bus and about forty-five minutes later we stepped off at a gate on the edge of the Virginia Beach Naval Air Station. As the bus pulled away and we stood in the familiar smell of the diesel exhaust, a flood of memories washed over my mind. Several years had passed since I stood at that gate. This base had seen my 20th and 21st birthdays in the early 1970s. A ship exactly like my old floating grounds sat out there beyond the buildings and the clusters of barracks and warehouses, out of our sight. We had to walk a long way to get a view of it.

We requested visitor's passes and strolled onto the base. I easily remembered the route to the dock area, and for about thirty minutes we walked together down the streets lined with military signs and buildings that were mostly gray in color. Finally, off in the distance, we saw the silhouette of the great carrier. The kid's jaws opened in amazement at its ominous size, but my thoughts went to the lonesome feeling that had engulfed me when I walked alone down that street. My home in West Virginia and the distant woods where I loved to go and hunt had seemed so far away. I had felt so torn between wanting to return home yet dreading to because of the spiritual condition of my life. While on that base, I was as lost as the proverbial goose in terms of my fellowship with Christ. I had entered into my own "dark ages." I had longed to go home to see my folks and my friends, but I avoided the trip whenever I could in order to hide my sad state. Now, mixed with the excitement of showing Nathan and Heidi the wonders of naval technology that sat at the dock in the distance, I felt a deep sadness that my time in the Navy hadn't been more meaningful. But as I walked between two of the best and sweetest people I'll ever know, the flesh of my flesh, my heart began to fill with an overwhelming sense of gratitude that God had somehow brought me back to His love and light. And instead of my arriving at a destination of total sorrow, He had delivered me to a path of joy.

As we drew closer to the massive ship with its towering island and fleet of jets parked on the flight deck, the kids nearly jumped out of their shoes in awe. To their left lay a row of smaller ships and even a few submarines. Their little eyes bugged at the scene. In the quiet of my soul, I prayed a prayer of thanks to my Heavenly Father that He had allowed me the moment. Slowly, the emotions attached to the past gave way to the thrill of the present, the excitement of showing them the awesome machinery floating at each dock.

At last we stood near the bow of the great carrier. Nathan and Heidi literally had to look straight up to see its huge anchors. The forward portion of The Saratoga loomed over their heads like a friendly, gray monster. Their young hearts were beating wildly at the sight.

As we stood there gawking, I knew the kids must've been wondering how the sailors could go about their duties without turning often to also gawk at their enormous home. I too was re-amazed at the gigantic-ness of the ship. To this day, I wonder how on earth it can even float. However, I recalled how mundane it became in the nearly two years I was aboard The Forrestal. One does get used to its size.

I pointed out to the kids the aft, or rear portion, of the ship and showed them where I slept. Then I pointed to the section where I worked in the arresting gear division. The elevators that moved the jets from the flight deck down to the hanger bay were nearly the size of our church parking lot. Nathan and Heidi were quite impressed, to say the least.

Something at the dock was different from when I had been there, in my whites and wool blues along with that funny-shaped, round hat, in the early 1970s. Now the dock was fenced and visitors were not allowed to go near the gangplank nor board the carrier. I stopped a young, passing sailor and asked him if visitors were ever, under any conditions, permitted on board. He informed me that only if they were family. For a moment my heart sank. Then I got a mischievous idea. In order to tell about it now requires a confession.

I so wanted to get my kids aboard the carrier so they could see the insides that I folded a $20 bill flat against my palm, shook the sailor's hand and said, "Could I be your uncle for an hour?"

Without hesitation that young salt made a sinner out of me! (I found out later that the rules were much more relaxed than I had been told, and that with some fancy talk I probably could've avoided a need for repentance.) At any rate, within two minutes we were all standing in the belly of the great ship.

The young man showed us his home, stem to stern. When the kids saw the tiny room that was exactly like the one where I had lived, and heard that it housed seventeen men, they were shocked. How could anyone sleep in such close quarters? In fact, I wondered too how I ever did it!

Before we left the ship, I asked our young host if he would take us up to the flight deck. He agreed and up we climbed. Ladder after ladder, we finally reached the expanse of the flat deck atop the carrier. Carefully, he walked us to the edge and the kids gasped as they looked over the side to the water far below. It was frightening, once again, even to me. I could not imagine how it made Nathan and Heidi feel to see such open heights. We stood there looking down at the small figures of the dock workers and the on-duty sailors. I took advantage of the brief opportunity and began to tell the kids about the day we arrived back at the same dock following a six-month cruise.

We had departed in January of 1971 with a crew of 4500 men, and after touring the Mediterranean Sea around Spain, Malta, Italy, France and Greece, every seaman was extremely anxious to get home. The married men missed their wives and kids, the single men longed to see their girlfriends, and the rest of us were just plain homesick. Coming back to America was a momentous occasion for us all.

On the scheduled day of arrival we all decked ourselves out in our best dress uniforms, every hair was in place (what hair we were allowed to have), and we were smelling so good! I recounted to the kids my feelings as the dock, a tiny spot, came into view way off in the distance. Its dimensions grew with each mile we covered across the bay. Suddenly, we could tell that the dock was alive with people. More than that, as we got very close, we saw that it was packed with thousands of families and friends, waving their hands and home-made "Welcome Home" signs. The sound of the crowd swelled as we drew even closer. There must've been 10,000 people on that dock.

I told the kids that a month before our arrival, my folks had notified me by letter that they would be there waiting for me when the ship came in. One "old salt" who had been through the experience many times warned me that I might have a very hard time spotting them. The dock was longer than the boat and finding my family among the myriad of faces that would be below could take some time. I sent a letter to my folks saying I would bring my guitar to the edge of the flight deck. They could look for me as I held it by the neck and waved it. Silhouetted against the sky, I should be easy to spot. Then, they could work their way toward my area and I would look for their cardboard sign.

It worked! Within a little while they found me and I saw them. Their faces glowed in gratitude that their son, who had been away for so long, had returned to them safely. What a happy reunion it was!

The kids loved the story and as we made our way back to the gangplank and descended onto the dock, I thought, *What a great way to spend a day with them! We were able to get out of the hotel room, go outside, and make a memory.*

As we walked away from the huge ship, and the cool sea breeze whipped across our faces, I vowed to tell the kids someday about another time I returned home. That would be the account of the time I spent adrift on the dangerous waters of sin, and how God, in His great mercy, brought my sad vessel to the safe harbor of His love. That story, I knew, would also include the joy I can clearly remember on the faces of my mother and father when their son had sailed home . . . to Christ.

7

Seven Days of Incredible Bonding ... to That Seat

I'll never forget what I heard a dad say about the bicycle in response to an invitation to take a ride with his kids. He sighed deeply and said, "It's silly to pedal your legs off just to give your fanny a ride!" Perhaps there's a lot of truth in his assessment of a vehicle as ancient as the bicycle. Still, in my heart, there's a love affair with that two-wheeled wonder that spans most of my years.

I was about twelve when I finally raised enough money to get a Schwinn. It was a used, blue and silver beauty. My favorite part of that bike was the shock spring mounted to the front wheel at the base of the handlebar stem. That bike floated on a cloud down the bumpy streets. The rounded covers over the sleek center bars of the upper frame resembled a motorcycle fuel tank and gave the bike a strong and sturdy look. I was proud of that machine. The large tires safely hugged the pavement when I screamed down the long hill on Jericho Road near my house. Though it has long rusted away, that bicycle is still in my blood. Whenever I see one of those $1200.00 replicas of that particular model, I'm sorely tempted to partake. Someday I'll find one I can afford and I'll snatch it up, perhaps for a grandkid.

I'm not sure what it is about the bicycle that does it, but when I throw my leg over the seat and climb on, I'm a kid again. Perhaps it's the self-powered ride I enjoy. Maybe it's the defiance of gravity I accomplish when I take off without tipping over. Then again, maybe the wind in my face reminds me of a time in my life when the cares of life weren't so many. Whatever it is, I am still drawn to the bicycle with some regularity.

When the winter of 1989 came I began to toy with an idea I never dreamed would interest me in regard to the bicycle. My thoughts turned to the mystique that goes with an extended multi-day ride. As I pondered the possibility, I slowly became convinced that it was something I wanted to attempt. I began to look longingly at touring bikes, pannier bags, and other equipment required for a long ride.

Then in the latter part of the winter of 1990, thanks to too many 5K's, 10K's, a half marathon, and a whole one, I had to have knee surgery. After successfully struggling through re-hab, I finally resolved to the fact that long aerobic runs on the hard pavement were a thing of the past for me. By early summer, the bicycle had become my best exercise friend. One afternoon during a twenty-mile cruise through the countryside, my mind went back to the "long haul" idea from the previous year. Before my mind could tell my post-operative knee that it was too old to do it, my heart had fully committed to a serious trip. I decided to ride from Nashville, Tennessee, to Point Pleasant, West Virginia, where my folks lived. The trip would be around 425 miles and I planned to depart on July 31st.

While on one of my early training rides, another idea came to me that at first I rejected. "Take Nathan with you on the ride to West Virginia!" Initially, I thought he was too young and that it would be much too dangerous for him. Plus, I assumed Annie would never agree to it. However, when I presented the idea to Nathan, he immediately reacted so positively I knew he'd have to go with me. Annie was indeed reluctant to agree, but knowing that men will be boys, she decided to trust me with our son's life on the back roads of Tennessee, Kentucky, Ohio and West Virginia.

Nathan and I trained consistently. We knew that we had to prepare our legs as well as toughen up our backsides for the seven-day grind. We did thirty and forty mile rides at least twice a week and added several short trips.

As our departure date grew near, we were on a conditioning ride about fifteen miles from our house when Nathan presented an idea that I thought was excellent. He said, "Why don't we use this trip to raise some money for Alfred and Jean McCroskey's ministry to Russia? Let's get as many people as we can to donate a penny per mile and give it all to missions!"

So, we did. We made up flyers and enlisted several friends and family to donate. I was proud of Nathan for thinking of such a great idea and as a result, over $2000.00 was set to be collected and sent to the McCroskey's organization called Bibles For Russia. Because so many people had become involved, there was no way we would back out of the trip.

July 31st finally arrived. Our bikes were fully packed and weighed in at about 35 extra pounds each. We were ready. We were pumped. On the morning of our scheduled departure, Annie and Heidi took off for Pennsylvania. They planned to pick up Annie's folks for a visit to the Amish country, then rendezvous with us seven days later in West Virginia. They left our house at 5 A.M. Two hours later Nathan and I pedaled away from the comfort of our own beds and the cool of the air conditioning.

Twenty miles down the road, I looked over at Nathan as we struggled up a long hill northeast of Nashville and said, "Well, it's not too late to turn around. What do you think?"

His response was a resounding, "Let's keep going!"

That day we rode slightly over sixty miles and stopped just above the southern border of Kentucky. It felt good to have crossed into another state. I had mapped out the first day's ride for us over the safety of the remote back roads. We completed it and we welcomed the rest.

That night in our cheap motel, we were visited by several species of spiders and other creepy crawlers. It made for a tentative night's sleep to say the least. Before we finally turned the lights out, we agreed that because of the high caloric output we experienced that day, we were free to feed our craving for a late night snack. We hurried up the road to a small convenience store and bought a box of raisin bran and a half gallon of milk. As Nathan sat on the bed and chewed his first crunchy bite, he looked into the bowl and noticed the cereal was moving. He immediately started gagging, spitting, and spraying milk-soaked bran across the room. In total disgust, he announced that the cereal was full of tiny worms. He held his stomach as he thought of how sick he'd probably be. I assured him that the protein content in worms would be beneficial for his long ride the next day. He didn't buy it . . . but I'm grateful to report that the worms didn't affect him and when morning came, we were able to journey on.

The next six days were filled with non-stop memories such as gallons of Gatorade, demanding head winds, rude motorists, relentless hills, pizza, rest stops, dangerous down-hills, semi-trucks, and dreams of a bicycle seat that was bigger and softer.

One other item that needs to be added to the memory list provided one of the most unforgettable moments on the trip. It was the encounter with the dogs!

We had climbed a steep hill on a secluded back road in central Kentucky. When we reached the top, we were barely rolling and both of us were panting for breath. As we crested the hill, just before we began the relief of the descent, I looked across the yard to my right and saw a little white frame house sitting about 75 yards off the road. It had a high front porch and underneath the porch was a group of dogs. Because of the bank along the road, I was eye level with the critters and all they could possibly have seen was our heads bobbing along. Still, they stood up and took off toward us the instant they caught sight of us, all of them. The thought of the carnage they were about to create was frightening and instinctively I yelled to Nathan, "Get your *Halt* ready and prepare to sprint!" (*Halt* is the brand name of a small can of self-defense pepper spray designed for dogs . . . and rednecks!)

The barking beasts came off the bank and onto the road, and for some reason they ignored me and darted in front of Nathan. In the excitement of the moment, he shot a stream of pepper spray over his handlebars, straight at the dogs, and he pedaled for his life. He didn't realize that his forward motion would carry him right into the residual orange mist that hung in the air. In essence, he had just maced himself. He began to gasp and grabbed his face with both hands, leaving the handlebars at the mercy of the road. Off into the ditch he went.

What happened next was remarkable. I assumed that both of us were about to become Kibbles and Bits. Instead, all three of the dogs rushed over toward Nathan. As he wiped at the pepper-induced tears and scrambled to get up off the ground, he discovered that the dogs had stopped short of where he had fallen. They just stood there, staring at him, as if they were apologetic for causing the accident. They seemed to want to comfort this unfortunate stranger. Nathan quickly maneuvered his uninjured bike onto its wheels and, although the road was a blur in his sight, he rode. We both were very happy to still be among the living.

Now, while we were grateful for the mercy the dogs had shown in letting us pedal away, and though we were able to laugh later about the incident, we never did care for the threatening sight of dogs again. We confess that "revenge" was on our minds, but we never got another chance to make a dog sneeze or gag.

We pressed on until, finally, day seven came. All summer we had talked about the final day's ride. We dreamed and talked about the moment we would sight the "big blue bridge" that crossed over the Kanawha River into my hometown of Point Pleasant, West Virginia. We knew that, when we saw it, we would be near the end of our journey. When at last it came into view that day, our tired legs seemed to gain new strength. We were met at the end of the bridge by a patrol car and my dad was waving from the passenger's side to follow the officer across the bridge. We actually had a police escort into town! At the other end was a sizable crowd that included family, friends, and the local newspaper photographer who gave us front page coverage the next day. We had calculated our arrival at the bridge at about 2 P.M. and it was ten minutes past when we climbed off our bikes and kissed our family . . . and the ground. What a trip it was! Seven days of incredible bonding . . . **to that seat!**

Today we're still basking in the glow of the accomplishment. It's one of our most unforgettable adventures. And as his dad, I am grateful for one particular benefit Nathan gleaned from completing such a long and strenuous ride. It was the valuable lesson in what it means to set a goal, count the cost, and remain faithful to the end. That seed of wisdom has born good fruit in his heart. I was privileged to see it one day while we were working in the studio on a new album of songs. At a mere eighteen years of age, Nathan had been granted the responsibility of the "producer's chair" for the project, and the pressure was on. While we hope the end result will be pleasant to the ear of a listener, most people do not realize how grueling the recording process can be. It's long, costly hours of performance that require intense concentration and can be terribly taxing on the mind and emotions. When we were about 95 percent finished, we were sitting at the mixing console with our heads bowed in angry frustration with some recording machines that were acting weird. Also, a deadline stared us in the face the way those hungry dogs in Kentucky had looked at us. That's when Nathan looked over at me and said, "This hasn't been easy, dad, but I think the *big blue bridge* is in sight!"

How my heart melted when he said those words. In that moment I realized that spending seven days outside with my son . . . on a bicycle . . . had resulted in an important insight that would last the rest of his life. Was it worth the pain this "over forty" old man endured on that little seat? You'd better believe it was!!

(P.S. Since that ride in 1990 with Nathan, there have been others. Most recently, Heidi and I ventured onto the Natchez Trace Parkway for a rainy, hilly, four-day, 240-mile glorious ride through parts of Mississippi, Alabama and Tennessee. We highly recommend "The Trace" as a great place for your first long ride. It's safe, scenic, and sensational! Please note, when you pass through Tupelo, Mississippi, be sure to stop and stay with our friend, J. J. Jasper. Heidi and I can assure you that he'll treat you right and send you on your way with a surprise in your panniers!)

8

It's Not Just a Game

In early autumn of 1988, our kids headed back to school. The summer had been filled with traveling and other activities, but one memorable thing we enjoyed was watching the Summer Olympic Games on television with Nathan and Heidi. We marveled at the talent and dedication the athletes had shown in their quests for the gold.

In the spirit of the "Games," the Davidson Academy Elementary staff decided to hold a field-day event during the first week of school. Designed to be pure fun for the students, it was a great way to help them adjust to the confinement of the classroom after being outside for the summer.

The events included a foot race, which Nathan entered. With his confidence level high, he stepped up to the line. The flag dropped to start the race, and our nine-year-old "Olympian-wanna-be" took off. Within moments his ego shattered; he came in dead last. For his efforts, he received the dreaded yellow ribbon which simply meant, "Thanks for participating!" Feeling devastated and embarrassed, he endured the rest of the school day's activities, and came home looking like a whooped puppy.

He told us about his miserable showing at field day, and we attempted to restore his wounded spirit with milk and cookies. The consoling crunch of the Oreos filled the silence for a moment, but then I spoke up and asked him, "Son, what do you think happened out there today? You usually run so well."

His answer revealed the problem.

"Well, dad . . . I did exactly what you showed me those runners did during the Olympics. Do you remember pointing out that they saved their energy for the last part of the race and then *kicked* at the end?"

"Yes," I responded, wondering why such a well-used method had not worked for my son.

"That's what I did. I saved up, and then really poured it on at the end! And look what it got me. This stupid yellow ribbon."

I asked, "How long was this race you entered, son?"

"It was the fifty-yard dash!"

I sat there in silence for a moment and imagined what Nathan thought when he saw the other boys blast away from the starting line. He must have assumed they were making a grave mistake . . . until twenty seconds later, when the race was suddenly over and he was still prancing down the track. I nearly chuckled when I realized he had misused an age-old runner's tactic designed only for long-distance races. However, pity overruled my judgment and I quietly looked at Annie. She was also hiding a smile. We didn't say anything for a moment.

Then I told him how astute he had been to plan a race strategy. We commended him for his gallant attempt, and we tried to assure him that soon he would be able to rise above the agony of defeat. Later that evening, we were happy to see our son slowly returning to his usual self. We talked about the fact that even in losing there is something to be gained—such as knowing how and when to use the "right" strategies in athletic competition. Eventually, he was able to laugh about his mistake and actually looked forward to seeing his friends the next day. It was good to see the light in his eyes again. (Either we had helped him recover or . . . the *Oreo therapy* had taken effect.) Today, in our attic, tucked away in one of our precious memory boxes lies a yellow ribbon, rescued from Nathan's trash can that night. Perhaps someday he'll want to show it to his children and tell them about a day he spent "outside" at school!

Seeing a child fail is never easy. The experience Nathan had that day not only yielded for him some priceless instruction about dealing with a last-place finish, but it also taught us something of great importance. Not much in terms of learning the valuable lessons from failure is transferred in the moments following a defeat. During that time after Nathan came home, too many waves of emotion pounded on the shores of his heart. The ships of wisdom just could not dock in his port during the storm that followed such a major setback. It was better to let him weather the gale-force winds of disappointment while anchored in the safe harbor of his parents' unconditional love. Sometimes, as parents, all we can do is stand by like a mighty lighthouse and project to our young loved ones the beam of a gentle smile that says, "I'm here!" Then, after the storm has passed, we can talk with them about it. To move in too quickly with advice can seriously undermine the priceless wisdom found in Proverbs 25:11. *Like apples of gold in settings of silver is a word spoken in right circumstances* (NASB).

My heart breaks when I see a dad unnecessarily scolding a kid when the child has made a mistake. Many a golden opportunity to show unconditional love has been sacrificed on the altars of anger and impatience. I have seen a number of examples of this tragedy first hand at a particular place that is supposed to be a playing field for kids. Instead, for far too many youngsters, this place has been a killing field where little hearts are permanently wounded by unkind words from insensitive dads (and sometimes mothers). That place is the baseball park.

Having a past connection to the game of baseball through my Little League experience, I can recall a few of my young friends who were brought to tears during our games. They sat in the dugout with their backs to the bleachers, and they dared not wipe the tears from their eyes brought on by their dads yelling angrily behind them. The dads demeaned those boys' best efforts. I've seen many a jewel crushed at the baseball diamond.

I never understood the verbal abuse that some of those guys handed out. All I knew was that the boys hated the last inning because they dreaded the ride home that they'd have to endure. And unfortunately, the ridicule was probably not confined to the ball park.

Win or lose, several of us always went to the nearby Dairy Queen afterward to celebrate the game, and some of the fellows were conspicuously absent from the treats. I felt deep sorrow for them. I can't help but wonder how they turned out in life. Perhaps some of them survived their rejections, but I have a feeling that the serious cases struggle even now with all sorts of crippling emotions.

For millions of dads, their outside experience with a child is concentrated during the spring and summer months at the baseball field. We have friends in Texas, Bobby and

Teri Price, who have four boys, all of them extremely athletic. The family has probably consumed miles of hot dogs and rivers of soda in their days at the diamond, and spent more time sitting on hard, dusty bleachers than anyone else I know. Their commitment to allow their sons the chance to glean the benefits of playing baseball is remarkable. And let me say, those boys, and their three lovely sisters, are absolutely some of the finest children we have ever known. Bobby does not tolerate laziness by any means. However, his willingness to let his boys deal with failure without beating them to a pulp emotionally has yielded young men exceptionally strong in character.

Some people say baseball is just a game. But I believe it's far more than that. It is actually an opportunity to show a child something that is eternal. Consider this timeless truth: Existing in the realm of the spirit, unseen by the eyes of flesh, is our "Father who art in heaven." If our earthly eyes were suddenly opened and His awesome glory could be seen, it could be that our bodies would literally melt. (Sort of like the character in the first Indiana Jones movie who arrogantly stood by at the opening of the Ark of the Covenant. His face melted off when the presence of God was depicted as being released!) Could it be that we are promised a "new body" when we get to heaven so that we will be able to contain the indescribable presence of God?

One writer noted that God is not different from man in degree . . . but in kind. It's not as though He attained some higher state through good works or through re-birth after re-birth. Instead, God has simply always been different . . . sinless and majestic . . . and always will be, and there's nothing whatsoever we can do to change it. It forever will be so.

The Revelation of John describes the reality of His splendor in this way:

Immediately I was in the Spirit; and behold, a throne was standing in heaven, and One sitting on the throne. And He who was sitting was like a jasper stone and a sardius in appearance; and there was a rainbow around the throne, like an emerald in appearance. And around the throne were twenty-four thrones; and upon the thrones I saw twenty-four elders sitting, clothed in white garments, and golden crowns on their heads. And from the throne proceed flashes of lightning and sounds and peals of thunder. And there were seven lamps of fire burning before the throne, which are the seven Spirits of God; and before the throne there was, as it were, a sea of glass like crystal; and in the center and around the throne, four living creatures full of eyes in front and behind. And the first creature was like a lion, and the second creature like a calf, and the third creature had a face like that of a man, and the fourth creature was like a flying eagle. And the four living creatures, each one of them having six wings, are full of eyes around and within; and day and night they do not cease to say,

"HOLY, HOLY, HOLY, IS THE LORD GOD, THE ALMIGHTY, who was and who is and who is to come."

And when the living creatures give glory and honor and thanks to Him who sits on the throne, to Him who lives forever and ever, the twenty-four elders will fall down before Him who sits on the throne, and will worship Him who lives forever and ever, and will cast their crowns before the throne, saying, "Worthy art Thou, our Lord and our God, to receive glory and honor and power; for Thou didst create all things, and because of Thy will they existed, and were created" (Revelation 4:2-11 NASB).

Does that sound like any human being you know or have known in the past? Of course not! One of my favorite T-shirts in my arsenal of cotton-bound sermons is, "Two things are crystal clear. There is a God . . . and you're not Him!" Our God and Creator is far above us in form and in kind.

Realizing this truth, the mere glimpse of God's awesomeness that John gave in his revelation would make any dad wonder, "If this God is so incredible, then how on earth can I relay to my child that such an awesome God is approachable? And how can I possibly show my child His kind of love?"

First of all, to tell them how God is accessible, you can read to them the Good News in Hebrews 10:19-22: *Since therefore, brethren, we have confidence to enter the holy place by the blood of Jesus, by a new and living way which He inaugurated for us through the veil, that is, His flesh, and since we have a great high priest over the house of God, let us draw near with a sincere heart in full assurance of faith, having our hearts sprinkled clean from an evil conscience and our bodies washed with pure water.*

Also pass on to them Jesus' own words in John 14:6: *I am the way, and the truth, and the life; no one comes to the Father, but through Me.*

Your kids, and you, are fallen creatures because of the sin of God's first created man, Adam. But thanks be to God, you can experience the presence of His fellowship because of His Son. Jesus Christ made a way for us to go to the Father through death on the Cross. It is not by our works that we are "saved" but by the completed, unselfish work of Christ (Ephesians 2:8-10). Oh! What great love He showed us!

And how can we display that kind of unconditional love to a child? One answer to that question is found in . . . brace yourself . . . BASEBALL! Yes, you read it right. BASEBALL!! Through the ages, God has chosen to touch the flesh with His spirit in the most unlikely ways. He has used a sling and a rock, a talking donkey, loaves and fishes, and even spit! If He is able to use these things to reveal His love and glory, He is, by all means, able to use a ball, a bat and a glove. That's right! God can reveal Himself to your child in a myriad of ways, including a baseball game.

How can it be done? Mostly it's done after a kid fails on the field: a missed base, a fumbled grounder, a dropped fly ball that loses the game. These are fleshly pictures of the spiritual failure of man. And they can be just as significant to a kid. And . . . they are golden moments for a dad to seize and use to display God's kind of love found in Romans 5:8: *But God demonstrates His own love toward us, in that while we were yet sinners, Christ died for us.*

In my opinion, no other lyric ever written better describes the opportunities available for bleacher-bound dads to pass on eternal truths than Bob Bennett's, "Song About Baseball":

Saturdays on the baseball field
Me afraid of the ball
Just another kid on camera day
And the Angels still played in L.A.
I was smilin' in living black and white

Baseball cards and bubble gum
I think I've got a hole in my glove
Three and two, life and death
Swingin' with eyes closed
Holdin' my breath
I was dyin'
On my way to the bench

But none of it mattered after the game
My father would find me and call out my name
An ice cream, a sno-cone, a candy bar
A limousine ride in the family car
He loved me
No matter how I played
He loved me

But none of it mattered after the game
My father would find me
And call out my name
I was dreamin' of glory the next time out
But my father would show me what love is about
He loved me
No matter how I played
He loved me.

(Bob Bennett/Straightway Music/ASCAP/1982)

Any child fortunate enough to have a dad who responds to their failures the way the father does in this song, is blessed beyond measure and will likely never struggle with understanding and accepting the Heavenly Father. For all dads (and moms as well) who devote every free moment of their summers to baseball, remember to embrace the foul-ups your kid will inevitably have. Please, don't make fools of yourselves by sitting in the stands and inappropriately screaming at them. Instead, remember our God as described in John's Revelation and the fact that He sees you sitting in the bleachers. It's a sobering thought for sure, but it will help you keep in mind a truth about baseball . . . it's not just a game!

9

Mama Knows Best

Someone once said, "Hunt *with* a son when he is young, and you won't have to hunt *for* him when he is old!" Those words are rich with truth. In my relationship with Nathan, our hunting experiences have yielded many good memories, and some special times of deep bonding. I'm convinced that one of the results of our hunts together is that he will always be within heart's reach—no matter where he is. We will always be close.

Some of our experiences are told in the book, "*A Look at Life from a Deerstand.*" The following is one addition to the list of lessons Nathan found in the hunter's woods. It resulted in strengthening not only his personal character, but also his relationship with his mother. Ultimately, it also yielded a life-changing song lyric for both father and son.

It happened on a morning he climbed into a treestand before daylight here in Tennessee. Around 7 A.M. he heard movement behind his tree. Slowly he turned his head and caught sight of a large doe to his left. She stopped, but he could still hear the footsteps of other deer. He realized other whitetails were around him and he shifted his eyes carefully to find them. As he searched the woods, the rustle of leaves directly below his stand caught his attention.

Slowly, he looked down and straight underneath where he was sitting stood a young fawn. Then another appeared.

His heart was racing with "buck fever" and the two yearlings had no idea that a human loomed above them. However, mama deer knew something wasn't right. Nathan wasn't sure if she picked up an out-of-the-ordinary odor or if it was simply a sort of sixth sense that deer have to detect danger. But for some reason, the mother deer came to full alert.

Instantly, Nathan noticed that the young deer became nervous as well and they fixed their gaze on their mama. If she moved, they moved. If she sniffed the air, they sniffed the air. Not for a second did they take their scared little eyes off of her.

The doe stiffened and stomped the ground with one hoof. Nathan sat motionless, knowing that the slightest movement would ruin the morning. Only the fawns' ears twitched. They were afraid, but they were "in school," learning the ancient art of survival.

For several minutes, Nathan watched as the heritage of animal intelligence was being handed down to the young whitetails. Eventually, the two inexperienced deer left the woods, still alive.

Nathan later voiced a very insightful observation. Neither of the fawns dared to challenge their mother's astute sense of peril. He said, "They [the two fawns] didn't look at each other and mock their mama. Nor did they run off in defiance of the older deer's wisdom. The two young students never said, 'She doesn't know what she's doing! Let's go play!' Instead, they paid very close attention and as a result, they lived to tell about it." What incredible perception on

Nathan's part. I was amazed. He had gleaned an invaluable lesson that all young humans should learn: It's foolish to ignore the seasoned instincts of parents.

Not too many months after that morning, Nathan referred to the experience in the treestand. It happened after an incident took place between him and his mother. He came face to face with the stomping of her foot which indicated that danger was present. We had boarded a plane in Minneapolis, the second leg of our flight to Montana. One of the male flight attendants was unusually effeminate and displayed strong homosexual characteristics. Nathan began to make fun of the man, mocking him and generating a lot of laughter from Heidi as well as other passengers. Suddenly, Annie turned around and looked over her seat back at her, or *our*, mischievous son and offered him a stern rebuke: "Nathan! Do you realize that while you're laughing at that man, God is crying about his sad condition?"

Needless to say, a hush fell over our seating area and Nathan was speechless. So were his dad and sister. We were quiet for several minutes. None of us looked at each other. Unadulterated truth has a way of doing that to us. It basically shuts us up! We were stunned.

When we landed in Montana and went to our motel, Nathan secluded himself in his room to lick the wounds in his ego. We prayed for him as he worked through the embarrassment he had suffered on the plane. The next morning, during our drive in the rental van to our final destination, Nathan took his guitar out of its case and asked us if he could sing a song he had written the evening before. During his quiet time in the hotel room, he had penned the following words to a song he entitled, "While I Laugh."

While I laugh, God cries
See the tears in His eyes
My side is aching
His heart is breaking
While I laugh . . . God cries
Oh God forgive me my sin
Making fun of other men
I'm making light
Of a horrible life
Soon they will die
May I never again
Be a mocker of sin
What I say when they leave
It will be laid at your feet
May I see every sinner
With a heart full of pain
And may I always remember
If I dare to mock their shame
That while I laugh
God cries
See the tears in His eyes
My side is aching
His heart is breaking
While I laugh
God cries

(Nathan Chapman/Times & Seasons Music/
BMI/1996)

We were deeply moved to learn our son had responded
to Annie's reprimand in such a gracious way. The lyric he
had written was his admission that his mother was correct

in her assessment of the situation. It also was his confession to his heavenly Father that he had been in error. Our young deer had learned a great lesson from his "woods-wise" mama. The other young fawn, along with the daddy buck in the family, had also gleaned an important, life-changing insight. As a result, to this day, none of us have made fun of those who had once been the victims of our mockery.

That evening in concert, we asked Nathan to sing the song he had written. He prefaced the performance with the background of the lyric. Others were moved to the same conviction captured in his words, and they approached him after the concert. They strongly encouraged him to continue singing the song. We eventually recorded it on our "Never Turn Back" CD. Later I pointed out to him that a rebuke, when rightly received, can yield positive and eternal results. And a right response can have a positive effect not only on the one corrected, but also on those who see the outcome.

If you go to the hunter's woods with your children, always keep in mind that there's a lot more to find *out there* than just deer, turkey or squirrels. If you'll keep the eyes of the spirit open, you'll find some awesome truths. And be careful to let your young fawns know that many times . . . mama knows best!

10

The Dreaded "Y" Word

On the list of all that my children and I have done together in God's great outdoors, the following is not necessarily a candidate for the "enjoyable" column. Most folks do not look forward to this classic adventure, nor do we look back at it with fondness. This particular activity has yielded some of the best results, but unfortunately, it didn't take us to any faraway places like Canada or Alaska. It held little, if any, mystique. It was mostly dreaded, yet, we regularly returned to it. It was . . . YARDWORK!

I distinctly remember as a kid the depression I felt when the dreaded "Y" word would fall from my mother's lips. It was like a prison sentence without the possibility of parole. Oh how my countenance would drop when my mother mercilessly called to me as I was lying like a slug on the couch in the heat of summer. "Steve! Get out there and trim the sidewalk! We've got company coming! You know where the scissors are. Now get to it!"

The pre-modern-era weed-eating tool she spoke of was her pair of heavy, retired sewing scissors. Once upon a time, they were a shiny, precision instrument used to cut cotton for her homemade dresses. After they became dull, rusty, and loose at the hinge, she demoted them to cutting the grass that hung over the edge of our front sidewalk.

I mumbled my reluctance to the task, but I knelt down on the pavement and started snipping away. If the scissors had been made for the left hand, I could have knelt on the soft dirt that lined the sidewalk. However, being right-handed required that I put my bony knees on the lumpy concrete. Groaning and complaining the entire distance of the walkway, I would carefully clip every green ribbon that protruded past the prescribed edge. I did not want to repeat that journey on the rough surface, so I made sure every blade was reduced to a nub.

Finally, I would stand to my feet and look back at my handiwork. I rejoiced when I could announce to my mother, "I finished it." For two weeks, I would not have to suffer through that again.

Though it was a drudgery to perform, a certain joy usually awaited me at the end. The pain that throbbed in my aching knees and tired hand seemed to disappear when my mom stepped out on the front porch and said something like, "Oh! Fine job, son! Looks great. I'm proud of you! Now our friends won't have to walk through a jungle to get to our front door! Thank you!"

Personally, I wouldn't have cared if our visitors needed to walk through a rain forest to get to our house, but I always felt grateful for my mom's kind words. The reward of her comments made me glad I had done the job. Perhaps her compliments were part of some clever ploy that moms and dads use to get work out of their kids. However, because I had been so careful with the trimming, I believed her accolades for me were genuine.

Many years have been clipped away since that rough sidewalk tortured my young, tender knees. Also, those heavy, cumbersome scissors have long since rusted out. Still, I carry with me the sweet memory of my mother's face as it "lit up" at the sight of my finished task.

Finally, it came my turn to pass the horticultural heritage on to my kids. However, my announcements of the work to be done in the yard never were delivered as easily as my mom's. I always issued the command with some depth of reservation. The main reason for my hesitation was actually selfish. I enjoy the work. Believe it or not, I love to mow the yard, dig in the dirt, and even trim the hedges. Something wonderful can happen out there when I'm working in the yard. For example, when the roar of the lawn mower overpowers every other sound around, I am left to hear only the sound of the song I may be singing or the prayer I may be offering.

Also, when one can hear nothing else in the ears, God can speak more clearly to the heart. At least two of the most important life decisions I have come to were made while sitting on a rider mower, circling the yard, and listening for that "still, small voice" to speak wisdom to me. For that reason, I am reluctant to give up my spot on the mower. Therefore, I make somewhat of a sacrifice when I ask one of the kids to do that particular job. However, when time was short and I needed the help, I would ask . . . and they usually obliged without resistance. I always hoped, by the way, that God would meet them there in the yard, the way He met me from time to time.

Some days, of course, the kids would grumble about having to turn off the TV and help outside. When they complained, Annie and I quickly reminded them of how easy they had it. Time and technology have carried us far beyond the old push mower and worn-out sewing scissors. Sitting down on a yard machine, graced with a powerful Briggs and Stratton engine, and turning a key to start the thing was a far cry from the back and forth motion of an open sickle, spinning between two hard rubber wheels.

Annie even resorted to reminding Nathan and Heidi of what she had to do to her front yard when company was expected. Because of kids and chickens, they had no grass, just dusty, soft dirt. When they expected visitors to stop by, her mom would yell, "Sweep the yard, Annie! Make it smooth as silk!" The broom would stir up a cloud of dust that drifted to the coffee tables inside the house, leaving more work to do. Nathan and Heidi didn't seem too moved by the story, but I thought it was pretty good!

As for trimming the sidewalk, there's nothing as nice as an electric edger. No leaning over, no crawling down an agonizing path of concrete. Zip! Zip! And its done! However, some of the joy in having such a glorious device gets lost in the dreadful chore of untangling the 50 feet of its extension cord. Nathan nearly convinced us that when we rolled the cord up and put it away in the garage and turned out the light, the cord crawled around and tied itself in tight little knots, just to torture us humans.

The occasional grumbles that quietly came from our kids sometimes made me wonder why they didn't appreciate the tools of our modern times. Then one day I realized that it would be hard for a present-day young person to appreciate the relative ease involved in lawn care when they had no way to compare *then* and *now*. Annie and I finally gave up on trying to draw the comparisons and resorted to simply issuing orders.

While "yard work is hard work," no matter what era of time we're in, I wanted the kids to glean one particularly valuable lesson from their experience. It was the same one I discovered as a kid. A job completed brings lasting joy. Where? Certainly not in the freshly mowed grass. That temporary happiness is quickly erased by a good rainfall and the passage of a few days. Within a short week, it looks like no one ever cut a blade! So, where is the *joy?*

To find it, I would take Nathan and Heidi to John 17:4 where Jesus says to His heavenly Father, "*I glorified Thee on the earth, having accomplished the work which Thou hast given Me to do.*" There it was! The reason for His joy. It was found in knowing that His Father in heaven gained glory among men as a result of a completed task. That result satisfied Jesus. Nothing else came close.

In the same way, when my children completed the work, I glowed with parental pride when someone said, "Your kids sure did a good job!" Nathan and Heidi could see my joy and it made them glad. If they got nothing else from the drudgery of working outside in the yard, I hope that memory will remain with them. For that reason, like my own mother did, I tried to always complement them and thank them for their labor. I knew they probably would not be able to "see" my pride—I had to verbalize it. And they were always grateful for my words of praise and thanks.

If you're a dad who presumes on your kids' hard work, whether in the yard, or in a family business, or wherever, let me encourage you to say, "Thank you," and, "Good job!" as often as you can. Until you do, how can they have the joy of knowing your pleasure in their completed work?

Admittedly, not all yard work will yield these kinds of results. Some days it'll be just sheer pain, followed by depression. Also, on other days, prying a kid off a couch will be like trying to pick up the Sears Building in Chicago and move it two blocks down the street. However, we found one tactic that seemed to get more help in the yard than any other. How many times have you heard your kids say these two dangerous words, "I'm bored!"? I think the last time Nathan and Heidi said them was around 1985.

I had heard it just too many times so one day, after hearing it again, I made a life-altering announcement. It changed their lives . . . and mine. I said, "Next time those two words, 'I'm bored,' are said, whoever says them will owe me ten dollars! That's right, ten big ones! Got that?"

It wasn't too long before I found some I.O.U.'s on my desk. And where would the money come from to pay the fines? THEY HAD TO WORK FOR IT! Muttering moans against the management, they had to saddle up the Snapper, for example, and mow the yard. They moved firewood, dug ditches, washed cars, swept the deck, etc.

It worked! Within the span of one short summer, those two dastardly words were gone from their vocabulary as if surgically removed from their brains. This is not to say that the kids were never bored again, by any means. However, if they were, I didn't have to hear about it!

More important, I believe they learned that when the hazardous feeling of boredom begins to come on, it can be replaced with something more productive. Also, they discovered the virtue of self-control when they were tempted to utter those costly words, and a little self-discipline has never hurt a kid! (By the way, I made about $90.00 dollars that summer from the deal. Did I give it back out of mercy? No way. I used it for school supplies!)

Of course, sometimes perceived "hard work" can deteriorate into glorious, unadulterated FUN! When the fall of 1986 arrived, the kids were nine and six. When the leaves started to drop from our oak and maple trees, they created a beautiful rust- and orange-colored blanket. However, the inevitable job of clearing them away began staring us in the face—the trees had yielded a nearly ankle-deep mess. When all the limbs were finally bare, it was time to go to work. Off to the back yard we went, Nathan and I with our rakes, and Heidi with the roll of black, plastic bags.

We pushed and shoved on the dry, crispy leaves until sweat poured off our faces. Two hours later, we had formed an impressive mound. All we had left to do was hope the wind would remain calm and get the leaves into the trash bags. Then we would be off to the dumpster. I stood under an oak, resting while leaning with one hand on the rake and the other on the tree. I stared at the mountain we had made and thought, "We're only halfway through with this job!" What a depressing thought! The kids were tired, and I began to entertain thoughts of moving to Arizona where people don't have this problem. I sighed. The reality of two more hours' work loomed over my weary mind.

I opened my mouth to announce that break was over and it was time to get back to our chore, when something from my faraway childhood reminded me, "What you've created here is not a mound of work—it's a mountain of fun!"

Without hesitation, I let the rake fall to the ground, walked over to Heidi, picked her up nearly over my head, and promptly threw her into the soft, noisy heap. Muffled by the leaves that engulfed her, she fought her way to the top, laughing and flailing her arms.

Nathan looked at me with that, "Hey, its my turn!" look. He didn't have to say the words—I knew what he wanted. Into the pile he went, and disappeared. Then, diving into my past, I went head first into the leafy cushion. Leaves flew everywhere, spilling back into the yard. Without apologies, we flattened the mountain. We grabbed our rakes and quickly reformed the hill. Over and over we took advantage of the autumn fun.

We did not know we were being watched. From the basement window in the laundry room, Annie, folding clothes, caught sight of the madness. She heard the kids screaming with laughter and saw me acting like one of her babies. She shook her head and continued to fold . . . then suddenly stopped, got a sweater, and did something totally contrary to her nature. She stunned all three of us when she walked up to our mattress of oak and maple leaves, turned her back to it, and free-fell into the soft bed. She laughed, the kids laughed, and I grunted each time I threw a child. We had a grand old time . . . even Annie.

I later asked my normally laundry-room-bound wife what dared possess her to forsake the unfolded clothes to go out and play. What she told me I'll never forget. "Steve, you know the loss of Donna Hummell greatly saddened us this summer." (Donna died of cancer at 37 years of age and left behind three small kids and her husband, Jim.)

Annie continued, "I stood there by myself in the laundry room, folding clothes . . . again . . . I saw you outside with our kids. At first, to be honest, it perturbed me a bit that you all were not working. Just a little jealous, I guess. But I suddenly thought of Donna and wondered, 'If she were here, and those were her kids and Jim out there, what would she do?' I knew she would've dropped whatever she was doing and spent some time making an enjoyable memory with her family. So, that's what I did. The clothes would wait, but the kids won't always be out there in the yard. I'm glad I did what I did. And to be perfectly honest," she added with a smile, "I did have fun out there! I can't wait until next fall!"

I knew that Annie worked very hard at maintaining our household, and her labor was extremely valuable to all of us. For that reason, I deeply admired her decision to take the time to go out and play. And, as a family, we made an important discovery that day. While it is great fun to journey to faraway places to find the "gold" in the great outdoors, sometimes diamonds can be mined just beyond the squeaky door . . . while doing yard work.

11

"How Much Feet Is It?"

One day we did it! Our family went out and bought that "hole in the water you pour money into!" We got ourselves a motorboat, a used 18-foot inboard/outboard with a "deep-V" hull and a Chevy 3.8 liter V-6. We equipped it with a stainless steel prop, and the dealer assured us it could easily do 45 mph across the water. We made our purchase in January of the year, hooked it up to our truck, took it home, promptly parked it in the garage, and began the long and painful wait until the ice thawed at our local lake. That year winter seemed to last forever. We thought late March would never arrive in Tennessee.

As the welcome signs of springtime started to appear, our excitement grew and we daily looked in the garage to see if our fiberglass friend was still there. Through the month of February, Annie and I often found Nathan and Heidi out in the cold garage, sitting in the boat with their sweaters on . . . pretending.

Finally, when the young tender foliage on the trees began to resurrect, we decided that it was our cue to come out of hibernation and take our water toy to Old Hickory Lake. Though the late March day was quite sunny, the frigid remains of winter left a crisp chill in the air. It felt a little odd to the kids and me as we donned gloves, sock-caps, and coats, pulled the boat out of the garage, hooked it to the hitch, and climbed into the truck. We had determined not to wait another day. Annie, who freezes in October and thaws in June, did the wise thing and stayed behind (to pray for us I'm sure!).

Their giddy chatter filled the cab as we drove along; obviously Nathan and Heidi were feeling only the joy of the day. Not wanting to spoil the fun, I worked hard to hide the intense fear I felt as the lake came into view. I was shaking on the inside with the same kind of anxiety one might experience just before a root canal. Seriously, I was nearly hyper-ventilating. Why? I'll tell you why. I had to *launch* that thing—that mound of money that rested on the trailer behind me!!

Before March ever arrived, I had made a few secret trips to our chosen ramp for the sole purpose of watching veteran boat owners go through the processes of launch and re-trieve. I observed the amazing skill of the lone boaters as they arrived at the ramp, jumped out of their 4-wheel drive monster trucks, removed their motor support brackets, detached this and that, checked if the drain plug was in, and skipped hurriedly and happily back into their trucks. Then, with absolutely no fear of losing their investment to the bot-tom of the cove waters, they would back their submersible trailers into the water and let their money sponges slide freely off onto the surface of the abyss, held in their posses-sion only by the thin thread of a tether line. It was a sight to behold. It had made me shudder in complete dread at the thought of performing the same feat someday. Well . . . that day had come. I was petrified . . . and the kids were elated.

How grateful I was to find no one at the ramp when we arrived. With my knees knocking, I exited the truck and tried desperately to remember my name and the names of my children. I held my forehead as I frantically searched my brain for the first step. Finally, it came. "Remove the motor support bracket . . . dummy! Now, check to see if the drain plug is in!" It all started coming back to me and I was doing just fine . . . until . . . there came the rest of the boating population of Davidson County to the ramp. I immediately decided they'd all just have to deal with my maiden voyage. If it took the rest of the day, or the week, I was going to do it right and make sure my garage would be re-filled with our boat when the experience was over.

As it turned out, things went pretty well. I did forget, however, to lower the prop section into the water before I fired up the engine. It sounded like a military jet passing over, and at least a few fish died from shock. Other than that, I did pretty well. I backed out into the cove and slowly headed toward the big water without playing "bumper boats" with the others who had joined us. That in itself was a major accomplishment.

The one-hour ride was incredible. The effective instruction the dealer had given paid off and I quickly got used to "coming out of the hole," trimming the engine, and maneuvering safely over the wakes from other boats. As we headed back to the ramp, my joy was quickly replaced by that churning fear in my gut when the ramp again came into sight. It announced to my fragile nerves that I would have to get our life savings safely back onto the empty trailer.

On my previous visits to the ramp to learn from unsuspecting others the art of launch and retrieve, it had seemed simple to reunite boat and trailer. However, on one of the three or four occasions, the wind had caused some slight problems with getting their vessels onto the trailers in good alignment. I had hoped I wouldn't have to deal with that challenge. But as fate would have it, the midday winds of March had moved in while we were out. We chugged slowly up the cove through the no-wake zone, and my blood ran cold at the thought of pulling into our driveway and Annie coming out on the porch to see the boat laying sideways on the trailer.

I wondered where the fun had gone.

Nathan held the boat to the dock with a line while I carefully backed the trailer down the ramp. With just the tops of the wheel fenders showing above the water, I mashed the emergency brake so hard I thought my foot was going through the floorboard. I definitely didn't want to baptize my truck.

I re-boarded the boat, fired it up, and slowly circled around. With the bow of the boat pointed straight at the front of the trailer I barely moved ahead in forward gear. Right away I knew I was being blown out of line by the wind whipping down the cove. I aborted the attempt and circled around again. I believe it was on about the fourth try that I decided it was time to put on my life vest, jump in the water, swim to shore, leave the boat, and just forget the entire deal. I would put plywood across the trailer and use it to haul mulch in April. However, I fought the temptation to abandon our ship and mustered a new determination to park it on my portable dock that was soaking in the lake. It was a chilly day, but sweat was pouring off my brow.

To make things a little more "memorable" for me, the kids made an innocent attempt at comforting me by yelling their encouragement. And, of course, their voices carried across the water like a broadcast over a rock and roll sound system. Every ear on the lake heard their calls. "Dad, you can do it! Don't give up! Don't be afraid . . . don't choke!!" I waved in appreciation for the attention I was getting . . . from everyone around.

I had no choice but to succeed with my reputation as a sailor and as a father on the line. I tried starting off center of the truck and timing it so that when I reached the rear of the trailer, I would be in the right position to ease up onto the carpeted supports that the boat would rest on. Sure enough, it worked, except for one misfortune. What I had dreaded had come to pass. I was sitting rather sideways on the trailer. I just about soiled my britches. However, I was not about to try again. I turned the motor off and sat there pondering my next move.

I decided to attach the line that secures the bow of the boat to the trailer, back a little further into the water, and man-handle the silly thing into the right position, then hand-crank it on up. It worked! Nathan and I were able to complete the job together and we danced in victory. I jumped into the truck, started the motor, mashed the brake as hard as I could, put it in low gear, revved the engine, and jerked the lever that released the emergency brake. I shot up the ramp in rapid fashion; the water fell away from the immersed trailer. I felt something scraping behind me and Nathan quickly informed me I had failed to raise the lower unit of the motor.

I left a mark on the concrete ramp that I'm proud to say is still there . . . with all the other scars left by "first-timers." Little damage was done so we hastily cleaned the hull, remounted the motor support bracket, pulled the drain plug, and happily pulled away leaving a trail on the cold pavement as the drain plug hole let the lake water escape.

Believe it or not, I actually looked forward to going back to that ramp. (Of course, I'm a fan of poison ivy, too! It feels so good when I scratch it!) Seriously, I didn't dread returning to the lake and facing the challenge. I knew that each time I did it, I would only become more confident. Being one who has learned to "eat the chicken and leave the bone," I chose to dwell on the good parts of the process and forget the bad. Before too long, I was one of the "experienced" captains that the frightened new guys came to watch from the driver's windows of their trucks. I'm sure they were impressed!

As the weeks went on, Nathan and Heidi grew increasingly comfortable at the thought of placing both their lives and the life of our "toy" in my sea-weathered hands. I knew we had us an item that would be the source of many an enjoyable day in the summer ahead. As it turned out, I was right. We thoroughly delighted in every opportunity to "put in" and "hang out" together at the lake. That summer, we proved that a watercraft truly can be a worthwhile investment. (Men, feel free to read this to your wife!)

When April came, Heidi became a "ten-ager" and Nathan had become a teenager. Their different personalities became vividly clear at the lake. Nathan was willing to try just about anything on the water—skiing, knee-boarding, tubing, you name it. Heidi on the other hand wasn't so adventurous. If you were to ask Nathan what things he remembers most about our lake trips, I have a feeling one of them would be the five words Heidi said over and over that drove him nuts: "How much feet is it?"

It took a long time for us to figure out why Heidi would not enter the water unless it was at least ten to twelve feet deep. We eventually discovered that she was convinced a man-eating fish lurked on the bottom of the lake. She believed that if we went out beyond the shallow waters, her dangling legs would not be food for the monster in the murk. So, before she would jump out of the boat to swim, tube, or whatever, she would invariably ask, "How much feet is it?"

We all chuckled at her unwavering inquiry. However, I never failed to answer her honestly . . . because her fears were genuine. No matter how much I tried to convince her she had no reason to be afraid, she still demanded that we play and swim in the deep water.

We didn't realize just how hard Heidi had to fight to overcome her terror. Every time we hooked up the boat and headed off to the lake, she had to fight the battle between a longing to be with her family and a nearly debilitating fear of the shallows. Over and over that summer she endured the chuckles that came at her expense.

I'm not sure what sunny day the light came on in my head about Heidi's war with the water. However, I finally realized she was actually gleaning an important lesson from the lake in terms of the strength it required to fight a panic. When my eyes finally opened to it, I admired her for her willingness to quietly face each battle between fear and fun. It would be terribly foolish for me to discount her belief in the great fish that didn't really exist. Instead, I considered her assumptions as very real. After all, I was once the little kid who was paralyzed with fear at just the thought of ever going anywhere near my grandparents' attic. Grandpa Chapman had warned all of us grandkids about "Ole Bloody Bones," the ghost of a Civil War soldier who lived up there. To me, there was nothing more true. With that recollection, how could I ever disbelieve Heidi's nemesis?

I decided to love both my daughter and her vivid imagination. When we left the ramp, I headed straight for the deep water. Still, even knowing we were right over the river channel, she would ask as she stepped up onto the edge of the boat to jump in for a swim, "How much feet is it?"

I would glance at the depth finder and answer with a smile, "45 feet, sweetheart!" At that, she'd dive in.

Over the next three summers of going to the lake, she gradually began to release her fear of the gargantuan fish that never did manage to steal her fun. Slowly, the question, once as predictable as the rising sun, began to disappear. Eventually, we sold the boat to make room for a recording studio we needed to build in the garage. Our trips to the lake have faded into the distant but enjoyable past. How-ever, more recently, as I have watched Heidi sail on other waters of life such as dating, decisions about entertainment, the challenges of college life, and friends she chooses, "that" question has re-surfaced. I have gratefully come to realize that while she overcame her childish fear, she didn't throw away her cautious nature. Before she jumps into the lake of life's decisions, she is one of the few wise ones these days who are brave enough to ask, "How much feet is it?"

12

The Lesson in the Pop Bottle

Amazingly enough, we made it to a second summer with our motorboat in decent working order and still able to float. I dinged the prop only a few times on rocks that hid beneath the waters, and the stainless steel held up well. By the time another long winter had ended, Nathan was actually eager to hear "Heidi's question" again . . . and again . . . and again! So was I. We greeted early June with joy. School was out and it was time to play.

During the year at our kids' local Christian school, Nathan had been invited to join the drum line in the marching band and in doing so, he met a new friend, named Joey. Joey's incredible percussion talent got the attention of our drumming son and right away they "hit it off." (Literally. They banged in rhythm on everything from door facings to the back of our car seats! By the end of the marching season, they had beaten us nearly to a pulp!)

With school out for the summer and no classroom time or field drills, the boys became hungry for adventure. I suggested we head to the lake without the girls and let me see if I could "dump" them off the tubes behind the boat. Within moments they appeared with towels and tubes inflated and ready to go. We wasted no time. Within an hour I was jerking them around the lake, having more fun than human beings were ever designed to have. As I bounced wildly across the wakes I made, I would look back and see two faces showing nothing but teeth. Their excitement brought smiles as broad as a yacht—they were loving it. They clung to their tubes as if their lives depended on them, and they probably did.

After about twenty minutes of plowing through the rough water I had stirred up, I decided it was time to take a break, rest ourselves, and let the waves die down. (Thankfully, we were the only ones on the lake. That's one advantage of traveling on the weekends and being able to go to the water only during the week. The lake was ours.)

I turned the engine off and Nathan and Joey plopped their arms over the side of their tubes in total exhaustion. They gloated in the fact that the "old man and his motor-boat" had failed to dump them. As we drifted in the gentle current, their happy conversation boomed across the lake. They were in summer-vacation heaven.

I decided to add to their joy by offering them a cold soda, so I grabbed a coke out of the cooler and yelled, "Heads up!" I gave the full plastic bottle a heave and it sailed toward them like a wobbly cannon ball. My intention was for it to land near them and they could get it as it floated to them. However, I put a little too much accuracy into my throw and it headed right toward them. As the bottle fell from the sky, Nathan put his left hand up to catch it. In its fall, it had gained weight and momentum. When it reached Nathan's hand, the white, screw-on, plastic lid hit with excessive force into the space between his middle and ring fingers and didn't stop until it had torn the web of skin that keeps the fingers from separating. When the bottle finally fell off his hand, it left an uneven split that was deep and ugly.

At first, Nathan thought it was just a good stretching of the skin. But when he looked closely, he suddenly began to scream in agony and panic. The flesh had opened all the way to the joint of the bones in the mid-section of his hand and we had ourselves a serious situation. Nathan started paddling frantically with his good hand toward the boat, while Joey yelled a report of what had actually occurred. His description was shocking. I quickly instructed Nathan to douse his hand into the lake to clean the cut. Then in mid-sentence it dawned on me that we were tubing just below the Dupont Chemical Plant. I changed my directive in fear that my son might have glowed in the dark for the rest of his natural life. I audibly said a prayer over the noise of the engine as I put the gear in forward and circled to the boys. Joey drew in the lines and helped Nathan into the boat. I looked at the wound I had inflicted on my boy and nearly gagged. We wrapped his hand in a towel and took our seats for the wild ride back to the ramp.

The no-wake zone is a sacred area on all lakes. There is a purpose for the rule. I knew one very good reason is so that those who sit relaxed on their vessels at the marinas don't end up in the water from the bouncing waves that toss them about. However, I had an emergency. I plowed through that hallowed zone doing at least 40 knots. People gestured to me like you usually see only on the highways when you cut somebody off. I screamed in their direction, "EMERGENCY, SORRY, EMERGENCY!!" It didn't seem to console them much. They grabbed their drinks and hamburgers and dove for anything to hold onto in order not to be thrown into the lake. Fortunately I was not ticketed. If I had been, I would gladly have paid it because my son was in pain! I was on a critical medical mission.

We arrived at the hospital in our swim clothes, dripping wet and frazzled. They took one look at the nasty tear in Nathan's hand and immediately admitted him. Joey and I sat in the waiting room. After a little while, he brought up a subject that gripped my heart. "Mr. Chapman, do you think his injury will affect his guitar playing?"

My face must have turned ashen (to match my hair!). I had not considered what damage may have been done to my son's fast-growing ability on the guitar. He had started lessons and was excelling on the instrument. His natural gift yielded amazing progress, and now that talent was in jeopardy. My heart sank in the dread of discussing it with Nathan.

Time went on and his hand healed nicely. When the wound closed, Nathan was able to swim with us but he had to avoid skiing and tubing any more that summer. By the grace of God, the skin re-formed between his fingers. The eighteen stitches left behind a visible, but not-so-ugly, scar. We were just happy to see him normal again. It took about six months for his grip and usage of his fingers to return. He was thankful he could take his place with the marching band on the field once again that fall, carrying his bass drum and sweating with the rest of the musicians. I was relieved.

By the time winter came and the football season was over, Nathan had gone back to concentrating on the guitar. One day he was working on some chords his teacher had given him to learn. The playing of these particular chords required some significant stretching of the fingers. We were delighted to see that he had very little trouble with the strange jazz formations. And we were impressed with the ease he seemed to have in sounding the notes. Suddenly, Nathan stopped playing. He looked up at us, held up his left hand, and smiled from ear to ear. He separated his index and middle finger from his ring and little finger and held them out toward us. "Do you see anything weird?" Sure enough, his hand was slightly deformed—the distance between the two sets of fingers was quite noticeable, a result of the soda-bottle injury. We immediately saw that for a guitarist, playing certain complicated chords is pretty difficult . . . unless . . . you have a long reach with your fingers. We rejoiced, knowing that what could have been a tragic ending to our son's guitar playing instead gave him a good, unusually long, reach.

To this day, we marvel at Nathan's skill on the guitar. Wherever he performs with us, his gift is a highlight of the evening. More important, we are also grateful that he has come to understand an important lesson in the scheme of things. He'll be the first to tell you that we are all at God's mercy when it comes to our lives. If we belong to Him, He allows only that which builds us up. He will not put things on us we can't bear. And finally, ". . . we know that God causes everything to work together for the good of those who love God and are called according to His purpose for them" (Romans 8:28 NLT). This truth is an enormously valuable one for all the days a person will live. Though I'm not happy to have been responsible for the disaster on the lake that day, I am glad we were able to be outside for a while where we found . . . a lesson in a pop bottle.

13

The Red

Even though we sold our motor boat to make room for our "garage recording studio," the desire for going to the water did not drain from our hearts. We considered finding a jet ski to meet the need, but there were four of us, and we thought it might be a little crowded on a vessel advertised as a "personal watercraft." How could we fill our longing for an occasional day of cruising on the lake?

To try to fill the gap somewhat, I submitted to something one summer day the next year. Little did I know it would turn my hair to a brighter shade of silver! We went whitewater rafting on the Ocoee River in southern Tennessee near Chattanooga. That day I made two trips down that stream of horror . . . my first and last. There is a picture in a frame at our house that shows my family and me, along with two of our kids' friends and our raft guide. Some sadistically industrious photographer had positioned his camera on the bank and snapped the picture at about the half-way point in our downriver trip. The photo shows us out in the middle of the cruel spray, descending over one of the thousands of gigantic boulders in the riverbed. Oddly enough, we were all looking toward the camera, smiling ear to ear. The looks on Nathan and Heidi and their friends' faces expressed the amazing ability of youth to ignore the peril and enjoy the thrill. If you look closely at the picture, you can see that my wide grin is actually a mouth screaming in uncontrolled panic. Thankfully, the roar of the river covered my desperate cries of fear and saved my reputation for adventure. I was not having a good time. Loss of life by drowning is not one of my favorite ways to spend a nice, sunny summer day.

Annie didn't care too much for the ride either. As for her smile in the picture, she was thinking, "I'll never have to do this again as long as I live!" After we reached our takeout point and dried off, she told me something I'm sure I'll never forget. When the raft jammed against the boulder, she fell out, and her ankle lodged between two rocks covered by the frigid water. While she was trying to free the ankle, she started rehearsing how she would explain to the public why she had beaten her husband to a pulp with a wooden oar.

Fortunately, we all survived, and we laugh about it now. Nathan and Heidi actually wanted to go back but Annie and I begged them to wait until after we're dead and gone, just so we won't have to worry about whether or not they'll return alive.

Hoping to find a more peaceful way to scratch the H_2O itch, I searched further for a water activity our family could enjoy. Also, having spent so much on the construction of the studio, as well as the equipment, I looked for a more affordable water toy. Then one day I got an idea. It came to me as I recalled an enjoyable trip Heidi and I had taken three years earlier.

We met with about fifteen other dads and daughters in mid-western Tennessee for a canoe trip down the Buffalo River. We had a great time. We camped the first evening, and early the next morning we put in for a day's journey on the river. The ride was tolerable for a dad who prefers non-life-threatening adventure. We paddled and drifted along some of the most beautiful banks in our state. Something about the simplicity of the canoe captured both Heidi's and my affection. The quietness of the surroundings and the maneuverability of the vessel provided a wonderful environment for a dad-daughter outing.

I fondly recalled the Buffalo River memory, so I suggested that the family invest in a canoe. We did. We purchased a 16-foot, hunter green, fiberglass rig with wicker-type seats and wooden oars. As it turned out, only Heidi and I eventually carried on the interest in canoeing, and the boat became a treasured friend to us, even though it took a pretty good beating on rocks and concrete boat ramps. Later, we obtained another canoe, made of a material that can best be described as "Tupperware on steroids." It was much more durable and it also sported a drink cooler and car-key storage-well in the mid-section. Eventually, we developed an interest in kayaks and now we each have the cruising type. (No way would I allow a rough-water kayak to rot in my garage!)

Our favorite place to go canoeing or kayaking is only a few miles from our home. It's a place called The Red River in Robertson County. We affectionately call it "The Red." We put in at a public ramp near Adams, Tennessee, and take out at Port Royal State Park. It takes about two hours to travel from one end to the other, and it is absolutely one of the most peaceful times two people can spend in a canoe.

Stories about The Red are interesting to hear. It is said that many years ago the farmers would build wooden floats, load them with crops to sell, and drift down the river to the Cumberland, eventually making their way to southern Mississippi. There they would trade and sell. They would then sell the wood from the raft and walk back on the Natchez Trace trail to their homes in middle Tennessee.

As we floated our way on the small section of The Red, we sometimes imagined what it was like to make that kind of journey. How slow a pace of life those people must have had. And how rough an existence they surely endured. It could not have been easy, but they had nothing of more ease for comparison.

We also enjoyed the incredible scenery along The Red River. The long upper branches of the huge overhanging trees nearly connected one side of the river to the other above us. Going down the stream seemed like floating through a tunnel. The sun hid behind the foliage except for a few wonderfully placed patches where brilliant light danced on the smooth surface of the water. The light also brightened the wildflowers gracing the banks in the springtime. It was a somewhat spiritual experience to see what the Creator had made. And enjoying it in the quiet of a tranquil waterway made it even more delightful.

Then disaster struck.

In March the alarms sounded in Robertson County, Tennessee. Word quickly spread that the weather conditions were just right for major tornado activity. We watched the TV weather reporters as they scrambled to alert the communities in our area to batten down the hatches. For several hours, nearly a whole day, we wrung our hands and prayed that God would protect us.

When the skies finally cleared, the damage reports started coming in. There was extensive devastation in our county and to the west of us. Fortunately, our property was spared the carnage. A few roof shingles replaced brought us back to normal. Others were not so fortunate. We drove around to see some of the destruction, and we couldn't believe our eyes. The sad part was that some loss of life had also occurred.

By the time mid-April arrived, the affected citizens were well on their way to full recovery. The signs of spring lifted all our spirits. Along with budding bushes and baby wildflowers resurrected from their long winter's sleep, the desire awakened once again in Heidi and me to go to The Red River for a canoe ride. We loaded up the rooftop rack on the car and made our way to the muddy ramp. Excitedly, we put in and started our familiar excursion toward Port Royal Park. All was typically beautiful and we basked in the warm springtime air. We didn't know that just ahead, we would make a startling discovery.

About half way through the trip, we paddled around a bend, and we looked down a long straight stretch of the river. We both gasped when we saw what had happened. Our towering tunnel of tree branches and foliage had completely disappeared; the river bed was wide open to the sky, as if ripped open like a wound that went to the bone. We realized that the tornado had torn away the protective covering of sycamores, oaks, and other types of growth. Huge trunks of battered trees were strewn all along the banks and in the water. It looked like a bomb had been dropped on The Red. The sight gave us both an eerie feeling—it looked surreal. We tried to imagine what it would have been like to be on the river when the twister raged through the gorge. What incredible noise and horror must have whipped past. Had it been a summer day, we could easily have been right in the middle of it.

A sad feeling also engulfed us. We knew that no matter when we returned to the river, it would never be the same. We had loved the tranquillity of The Red. Never again would we drift by that area and not think of the disaster nature can dish out, sometimes without warning. We could not ignore the marks high on the banks left by the flood that the torrential rains had caused. Somehow, the canopy that the trees had once formed had made us feel protected as we quietly drifted along. Now, with the sky fully visible, we felt somewhat vulnerable to the elements and the feeling was not pleasant. We considered finding a new favorite river to negotiate with our canoe or kayaks, but we have decided not to forsake The Red. We still go back to it as if we are visiting a friend who has been seriously injured. We have known too many good hours with it to desert it.

Given enough time, the river will again become the tunnel of escape to serenity that it once was. Until then, we will allow it to quietly remind us of an important truth that is found in the splintered trunks of the great oaks and maples lying dead along the banks. They tell us that on at least one unforgettable day, they bowed to their knees when nature trembled before the Mighty Creator. Heidi and I viewed firsthand what awesome power just one storm can contain. And if such unbelievable force is stored in creation, we can only humbly try to imagine what frightening strength the Maker of nature holds. Whenever we slowly drift under the open sky, along that section of The Red, we are drawn to look up and offer our own words of worship to the One whose hands hold all the power of our universe. And years from now, if we return to the river with our children, we can show them the visible marks left by the One who passed through the valley that notable day. Without fail, we will always drift silently and reverently by that sobering sight.

The phenomena of events like tornadoes and earthquakes battering the earth and its inhabitants clearly reveal the fragility of mankind. Nathan wrote a song about this subject and he and Heidi recorded it on a CD. She sings the words which her brother adapted from Psalm 77:16-18. As you read the lyrics, keep in mind the tragic discovery we made that spring day on the river, and you will understand how Heidi can sing the message with such deep feelings. As a result of our friendship with that stream, we have discovered two things. One, we have found a place where we can enjoy a peaceful, temporary escape from the busy-ness of life. And two, while we are there, we respectfully come face to face with a valuable reminder of the power of the One who created . . . The Red.

ONLY TREMBLING

The earthquake shakes the ground
The thunder claps its sound
And the lightning throws its arrows
And clouds' tears fall all around
Tell me why this happens
Why the earth is so unkind

All of nature's only trembling
Before The Lord Most High

Only trembling
Only bowing
On its knees before God
All of nature cowers
At His awesome power
Only trembling before God

But we all shake our fist
And go our own way
And we laugh at all that's holy
We use His name in vain
But shouldn't we take note
Of how the earth is so humbled
And listen to the sounds
As frightened ground rumbles

Only trembling
Only bowing
On its knees before God
All of nature cowers
At His awesome power
Only trembling
Before God
Only trembling.

(Nathan Chapman/Times and Seasons Music/BMI)

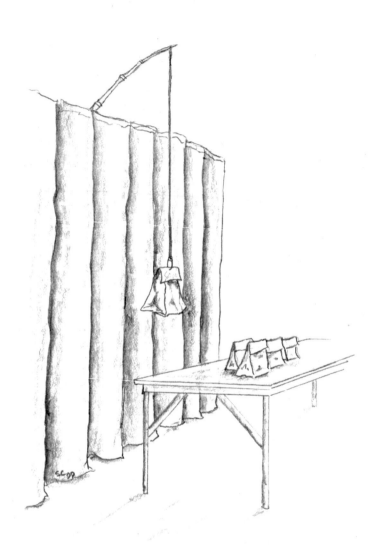

14

The Tug on the Line

My first fishing experience involved neither water nor fish. It did include a stick and a string, however. I was a little kid, at a church fund-raiser, standing in front of a six-foot-tall curtain made out of white bed sheets. My dad stood behind me—he had purchased my opportunity to cast the string over that wall of cloth. At the end of the eight feet of brown twine hung a safety pin. Excited, I held tightly to the bamboo pole and waited for a "bite." Suddenly, something jerked the line. I responded with a vigorous pull and my "catch" came flying over the top of the curtain! I held the pole as far away from my body as I could in my right hand and reached for the small paper bag that hung too far from my left hand—Dad grabbed it and pulled it to me. I handed the pole to him and excitedly detached the bag, reached in, and pulled out my trophy. It was a small plastic trinket, worthless to most, but to me, a whale of a treat.

I'll never forget the tug on that line. The thought that I had connected with something unseen and that it was about to be revealed was almost more fun than a little boy could stand! It must have been in that moment that my love for fishing set itself permanently into place.

Even today, whenever I have dropped a bait into the water, and the pole suddenly dances or the bobber disappears, a strange thing happens. Instantly, nothing on earth is more important for me to do. Work is suspended. Nothing else on the planet matters. All the world's economy could fail and I wouldn't notice. An asteroid could darken the sky and I would probably ignore it because something is down there going for my bait. And soon, if I do it right, it will be seen. An exciting pleasure accompanies every single tug of the line, without exception! Add to that the intense joy of a time of precious solitude found along a riverbank, or in a boat, and life hardly gets any better. No phone, no beeps, no hurry, no distractions. Unless . . . you take the kids!

If you've never fished with a child, you are yet to play with real danger. Like the lightning fast movement of a hockey puck that I'm yet to see on the ice at a game, I cannot see a fishhook in wild, uncontrolled flight when a kid is holding a fishing pole! Consequently, I've been the recipient of some barbs in the neck, in the leg, and in many a good shirt. But it was worth it. Besides, the blood loss has been minimal!

Once the danger years were behind us and it was safe to fish with Nathan and Heidi without losing an eye, we went on our first deep-sea fishing trip to the Gulf of Mexico. With Annie's permission, we booked a charter for a two-day, overnight trip out of Gulfport, Mississippi. After finishing a concert in Orlando, Florida, Annie headed to Nashville and the kids and I boarded a train for Jacksonville. It was our first ride on the rails. We stayed over-night with my Aunt Joyce Steele and then she took us to the Greyhound station where we picked up another brand new adventure (which we thought would never end), a bus ride to Mississippi.

When we arrived in Gulfport we were met by our friends, Randy and Linda Brownlee. Randy accompanied us to the dock at daybreak on a Tuesday morning and the four of us climbed on board a forty-foot fishing vessel, our first serious boat excursion. We headed south into the big waters. Within minutes of dropping our cigar minnows into the deep blue Gulf, we had a cobia (lemonfish) on the line. Nathan took his place in the chair and began the fight. For twenty minutes he pulled and reeled. Finally, the 42-pound brute came within reach of the retriever's hook.

Then before long, Heidi had her chance in the chair. We all helped her and for a ten-year-old, she did great, smiling the whole time. Of course, her cobia turned out to be the granddaddy of the trip . . . 51 pounds. Nathan offered his sister a genuine congratulatory pat on the back. The absence of jealousy in his heart made me proud.

The trip never took an emotional down turn. It was pure fishing fun. We flew home sunburned and glowing with some of the greatest memories a dad and two kids can accumulate. Now the pictures of us and our catch are carefully placed on the pages of a photo album that sits on a shelf in our home. They await a time in the future when another generation can hear about the trip.

Not all of our fishing trips have gone as smoothly. A return visit to the gulf with the Brownlees included a small disaster that merits telling. Though a less-than-perfect trip, it did yield a special bond between dad and daughter. Nathan was unable to go along, but Heidi and I, along with Randy, set sail in his 24-foot Seabird on a sunny August morning. After an hour of fighting choppy waters we reached the first oil rig. Randy moored to the east side of the structure and we began preparing to enjoy a morning of fishing for red snapper.

We had cut some bait when Heidi announced that she thought she saw a man walking around high above us on the platform of the rig. We had not seen anyone there on previous stops so we thought little of it and continued to ready our tackle. As we balanced ourselves on the deck of the rocking boat, I felt droplets of water on my arms. At first I thought it was condensation from the air conditioner that cooled the living quarters of the rig. Then I felt more drops. I looked up to see if rain clouds had suddenly moved over us. None in sight. The sky was blue. What happened next took place within a five- to seven-second span. I looked back at the bright white deck of the Seabird and noticed the falling water pellets were somewhat rust-colored and accumulating fast. All of a sudden, "something" fell out of the sky!

From the mid-section to the aft of Randy's newly restored, 1969 Seabird, the deck is open and uncovered for fishing purposes. We were standing right there, totally exposed, when unfiltered raw sewage began to pour down upon us. It came straight from the holding tank of the massive oil rig. The odd part of the moment was, as the "stuff" started to splatter on our heads and shoulders, all three of us looked up, gasping in stark horror . . . with our mouths wide open! What a mistake that was!

We quickly ducked under the five-foot canopy in the mid-section of the boat and looked back across the open deck. We saw brown spots everywhere on that beautiful, new white paint, plus a lot of yellowish liquid as well as a tint of the blue chemical fluid used in treating a holding tank.

The stench of well-ripened sewage gripped our nostrils, and all of us gagged in disgust. We looked at each other sort of laughing . . . the way you'd laugh in unbelief if the IRS arrived unexpectedly at your front door to seize all your property. As we exchanged blank stares, we saw it. Randy noticed that Heidi's hair was filled with chunky bits of "used manna." I saw that Randy's white T-shirt was spotted with brown marks. And Heidi observed that my pants bore the unmistakable marks of digestion. We all began to flail our arms and dance around the deck, "tip-toeing through the *turnips!*"

We had ourselves a crisis, the type that binds people together . . . if they survive it. Though we felt bonded, we were not about to hug! Randy quickly grabbed a water hose and started spraying Heidi, then me, and eventually himself. Suddenly, he realized that the pump supplying the water he was using came from the polluted area around the boat. We were only adding to the horror. We very quickly unhooked the mooring and powered away from that rig to fresher water.

Even though the water was salty and stung our eyes, we stood under the boat's shower, welcoming the rinse job we so desperately needed. As we changed shirts and mopped the deck, we began to discuss whether the "treatment" we had received under the rig was intentional. The speculation continued for a long while, and has even until today. Perhaps the fellow didn't know we were below him when he pushed the flusher button. Then again, we debated, just maybe he *did* know we were there. And maybe he took great pride in the patience he exercised waiting for us to position the Seabird in exactly the right place for his "bomb"!

Whatever the case, our dislike for that stranger grew as the minutes crept by. As we drifted and regrouped, Heidi and I discussed forgiveness following such an offense. Whether it was an intentional act or not, we knew we had to forgive the guy. It wasn't easy but we agreed to offer our pardon. Later, I took the opportunity to point out to Heidi that what happened that day unfortunately pictures what can happen in real life. Sooner or later, someone will "dump" on us, and if we don't learn to forgive and go on, all the joy in the journey may be lost.

I'll never forget what Heidi said about thirty minutes into our clean-up attempt. Not about to be deterred from our fishing trip, for which we had traveled so far from home, and from shore, to enjoy, my innocent 17-year-old said, "Hey! It's only *crap*. Let's fish!" Randy looked at me to see if I approved of her choice of words. I was a little shocked, but I immediately agreed with her. I realized the word she used can generate some controversy among some folks. But the truth is, any other word at the moment may not have been as appropriate. Somehow, "poo-poo" or "feces" just doesn't capture the essence of what happened. I think she used just the right word. But out of deference to those who may not agree, I will report that I submitted to better judgment in the situation and gave my daughter a gentle reprimand. I really was not ashamed of Heidi. Instead, I was impressed . . . and elated.

Forgive me, but I was overjoyed for two reasons. First, the past lessons I had taught her about perseverance in the face of adversity had somehow gotten through. Now we had one more twist to a familiar saying: "When the going gets smelly, the smelly keep fishing!"

Then second, it occurred to me that even though Heidi responded to a deep-rooted resolve placed in her by previous challenges I had provided, the real fact was—SHE LOVES TO FISH!! That, too, was a sweet revelation.

Fishing with a kid is also a wonderful way to help her (or him) "catch" one of life's most sought-after trophies—the assurance of their father's love. When a child knows of her dad's intense passion for "wetting a hook" and yet he chooses to take the child along, a transforming message is cast deep into the kid's heart. "Dad wants to be with *me!* I am worth his time. I am more important than a fish!" Those thoughts in a child's mind, when translated, say, "He loves me!"

Let me suggest that if you have younger children and you are contemplating the choice of including them in your next trip to the lake, be prepared not to fish. Instead, brace yourself. Resolve to the likelihood that, as alluded to earlier, all you'll get done is dodging barbs, baiting hooks, making sandwiches, pouring drinks, and wiping bluegill slime off your hands. Be patient. Don't yell. Instead, make it fun. Make a memory!

Finally, the next time you're at the water with a child and the hook is baited, the sandwich is in the left hand and the rod and reel is in the other, and the two of you are quietly waiting for a bite, don't forget to seize the moment. In that awesome time of anticipation, as brief as it may be, may I encourage you to consider the message found in "the tug on the line." It's a divine opportunity to tell your son or daughter about the moment when God tugs on his heart strings. Tell him that somewhere, below the surface of our flesh lies the deep pool of our spirit. And someday, someone unseen but very real will drop a line into his heart that will be baited with the purest of love. Let him know that the fisherman is the Holy Spirit of Christ. Encourage your child to accept the divine lure of His perfect love and become a trophy of the "greatest angler of all." Then, on another fishing trip, you can teach him about how He wants to make each one of us into fishers of men.

15

You Build 'Em ... I'll Fly 'Em

I bent over at the waist and planted my ten-year-old hands firmly on my knees. The nervous sweat from my palms made the leather of my fielder's glove damp inside. I was ready. Any fly ball or grounder that came my way was mine! I looked good in my off-white uniform, with the team name on the shirt front: LOCAL UNION 5668. I maintained the classic outfielder's stance and waited for the next pitch. Then something happened that I'll never forget.

Suddenly I saw it, in the air, just over the first-base bag, against the blue and white colors of the summer sky. The distant hum that came from its nose grew in volume with each passing second. It seemed to be headed directly toward me and I stood there in total awe. For the very first time in my ten years of existence, I faced a real-life, up-close encounter with the fascinating machine known as an airplane.

None of my teammates on the field, or on the bench, could have known how the approach of that fabulous metal bird entranced me. I had only recently arrived at the area and had not yet revealed my two-year-old serious interest in flying. Quietly, I was a "Chuck Yeager-wanna-be"! I just knew that someday I would make my living "at the stick." However, my desire for flight had been fueled only by pictures in books and occasional black and white Air Force movies. Living deep in the hills of Logan County, West Virginia, in a town called Chapmanville (you read it right . . . the roots run wonderfully deep!) afforded us only limited sightings of airplanes—on rare occasions and always too high to see the details. One gentleman, a mile or two up the river, owned a single-engine tail dragger, but I never did get to see him buzz around in it because he rarely flew it. It sat lifeless and lonely in a remote barn way across a field on the south end of town. Before I ever got a chance to beg to get near it, my dad took a job ninety miles away in Ravenswood, West Virginia, at the Kaiser Aluminum Plant. Our family of four packed up and moved. That day on the baseball field, in the rolling hills of Jackson County, for the first time I could literally read the numbers on the underside of the plane's wings as it passed over me. That created, to say the very least, an earthshaking moment for me.

Having been so surprised by the presence of the single-engine bird, my hands fell off my knees and hung lifeless by my side. I stood fully upright and gawked trance-like at the red and white machine. The Cessna screamed by, not more than 200 feet above me. My mouth gaped open, and I must have looked like one of the bluegrass-pickin' Darlin' boys from the Andy Griffith TV show. As I slowly turned on my feet to follow the sight of the plane, it headed north over the ball park.

Just like in the movies, when the scene calls for an audio trick where all the peripheral noise is eliminated and only one sound is heard, that's what happened to me. The only thing I could hear was the strong, deep-toned roar of that

Cessna's power plant. I stood with my back to home plate and basked in the glow of the flying spectacle. Suddenly the rest of reality began to "fade up" in my ears, and I was shocked back to the job at hand. The entire team and an angry coach were all screaming at me.

I wheeled around, looked to the infield, and saw someone running. It immediately dawned on me, "He's running to second base!" As he made his turn toward third, I looked at my dugout. All the teammates were jumping up and down, screaming my name. Then I saw the coach, walking quickly up the third base line, flailing his left arm and pointing at something with the other. Spewing tobacco juice, he yelled, "Wake up, Chapman! Wake up!"

I finally realized that a baseball lay somewhere near me. It had to be on the ground, buried in the nearby grass. I frantically began to search. I scanned all around left field and there, about three feet inside the foul line, near the outfield fence, I saw the top of the ball. I looked back at the runner just about to touch third base, and I knew there was no time for a play. I did realize, however, that I had to try to redeem myself by throwing him out. I ran as fast as I could but it seemed like the distance to the ball was a country mile. I finally got to it, picked it up, and heaved it as hard as I could. It took its first bounce just about two feet on my side of the third-base bag and rolled worthlessly to the catcher.

The coach threw both arms in the air, turned around and headed back to the bench shaking his head in disgust. The realization of what I had done horrified me. I was surprised I was not removed from the game. I supposed it was because only nine of us had showed up that day. Dreading the third out, I sort of hoped the inning would last until my adulthood because I knew what a tobacco-spit-slinging speech I was in for back at the bench.

And a good speech it was! The only thing I remember of what he said though was something I had never heard said to me, "Chapman, go home and take a cold shower!" I remember being totally bewildered by that statement. I couldn't figure out why anyone would ask me to do such a thing. "What did that have to do with the mistake I made?" I wondered. It was a number of years before I understood that the coach was trying to build into us a sense of teamwork.

The humiliation I put myself through that day did no damage to my interest in airplanes. I continued to build plastic models of fighter jets and I looked longingly at the pictures. I also hung around the ball field hoping to catch a glimpse of any of the small planes that took off from the local airport.

However, as it always does, time went on, and my boyhood dream of being a pilot never did materialize. Instead, my life began to be filled with other interests such as my role as a pastor's kid and becoming a musician for the church. Our family traveled around the area and sang together at churches. Along with that, a new love had captured my fancy. Thanks to one of dad's church members, Kenneth Bledsoe, I discovered the joy of being on the ground as a hunter in the great outdoors. After high school graduation in 1968 I went to college; later I enlisted in the Navy (and amazingly enough, I ended up on the aircraft carrier, The USS FORRESTAL-CVA-59). Discharge came in 1972, and in 1974 I moved to Nashville, Tennessee, to be a part of a Christian music group. In 1975 I married Annie and my role as husband became my chief interest. Then father-hood happened!

By the time our son, Nathan, was born in 1977, my thoughts went to a myriad of other things, and my dreams of sitting in the cockpit lingered far away in my past . . . that is . . . until one day in the summer of 1987. Nathan was ten years old when one day we drove by The Hobby Shop of Madison near our home. We had never been in the store and we decided to go in and look around for a few minutes. We browsed the aisles and did what little and big boys do in those places . . . we drooled . . . and then my eyes fell on an item that suddenly brought all those dreams of flying back to my heart like a homing pigeon: a wooden, gas powered, control-line airplane kit. My eyes lit up when I saw the man pictured on the big box. With the control device in his hand, he stood on the ground and, smiling ear to ear, he piloted the colorful, sleek, fully assembled bird. The look on his beaming face said, "Buy this kit and all your dreams will come true!" So, I did.

I took it home and assembled it as fast as the quick-dry glue would allow. Within a few hours I went to a nearby church parking lot to see if I was the "ace" I had imagined I'd be. Nathan went with me to be my ground crew. I squeezed the fuel out of the little can and into the tiny tank and instructed my son on how to start the engine. I stretched the two lines across the black asphalt lot and ner-vously picked up the control handle. My heart pounded with excitement when the small engine buzzed to life. At my signal, Nathan let go of the tail of the plane and it started rolling. It quickly picked up speed and I tilted the handle back toward me. There's no way to describe the elation I felt when the thing lifted off the ground and flew! I spun in absolute joy as I watched my plane race across the blurred background of our neighborhood. I was in aeronautic ecstasy . . . for about 30 seconds.

Suddenly, something went terribly wrong. The fragile little bird seemed to develop a mind of its own. It began to wobble erratically above the concrete. I panicked. I literally forgot all sense of reason. The state of utter confusion I entered alarmed me. I forgot my name, where I lived, and what planet I was on. I experienced complete shock. That's when I heard the "smack" of wood and aluminum on the hard, unforgiving pavement. I don't know what went wrong, but I was sure glad that I was standing at the end of those control lines and not sitting in the cockpit of my crumpled airplane! It was a mess. My new toy landed in a splintered heap and my heart shattered as well.

I was not about to be defeated, however! Believe it or not, I gathered up the fragments and rebuilt the thing. Two days later, we went back to the parking lot. Unfortunately, within seconds of the take-off, the same overwhelming sense of nothingness gripped my weak mind and lo and behold, I again drilled that baby into the pavement with a sickening thud. Once more, I collected the remnants and went back to my shop and rebuilt the bird. Before long, I was re-filling the tank and testing the engine. I couldn't believe it, it turned over and ran like a top. With some fancy glue work, we were able to return to our "airfield" a couple of days later.

I was filling the tank to try again when Nathan cleared his throat and spoke up. "Dad, do you think I could try to fly that thing?"

My first thought was disgustingly childish. The selfishness that welled up inside me embarrassed me. *This is my plane!* I thought. But, about a half minute later, adulthood returned. More important, my role as father won a great battle between my wants and my son's wishes. So, with only a residual of boyhood reluctance in my heart, I chose the high road and said, "Sure, son! You step over to the control handle and I'll start the engine. Give me a nod when you're ready." I instructed him briefly on what to expect based on what I had learned in my short-lived attempts, then flipped the little plastic prop with my index finger. It sprang to life and I felt the wind off the propeller wash over my arms. The volume of that miniature engine was marvelously deafening. What a wonderful sensation to feel the plane want to pull away from my hand. I had not realized how much I would enjoy that feeling.

I let go of the plane and it rolled away with its fixed rudder making it want to stay safely away from my young son. Nathan kept it on the ground for nearly a complete circle until I yelled as loud as I could, "Bring it up!" He tilted the handle and the plane was airborne.

Over the loud buzz of the engine I could hear Nathan screaming with excitement. The smile on his face was much larger than the one the man on the box sported. He carefully leveled the plane and never made another move of the handle until the engine sputtered from lack of fuel. The motor ceased to buzz and Nathan quietly and gingerly brought the plane down to the asphalt for a bouncy, but safe, landing. For the first time in its tormented life, our wooden wonder had completed a cycle. Nathan ran over to me and we danced as we high-fived each other over and over. It was absolutely a remarkable moment for both of us. I was as happy as though I had successfully flown the plane myself. And I loved being the mechanic!

The control lines of our aircraft started out in my hands and the result was disaster. However, in Nathan's hands it was much more safe. With his rapidly growing skill as a pilot, we managed to squeeze several more good cycles out of the plane that day.

On another afternoon, we returned to do it again. Eventually, Nathan just had to try a loop. After a couple more re-builds, he finally piloted his way into the ranks of acrobatic aces. Then a double loop resulted in still another glue job. As I patched the tired thing and re-painted it one evening, I decided to give it a well-deserved name. I used red and white paint (the colors of the Cessna that buzzed the baseball field many years earlier) and wrote the name, "9-Lives," on the top of the wing in honor of the repeated recoveries it had endured.

As I was putting the last drops of quick-dry glue on the tail section, Nathan came into the shop and we discussed our sympathy for the airplane. Then I said, "Son, I am resolved to the fact that you are the real pilot in this family. My talent for flying must've been erased by the aging process. But your mind is young and able to quickly sort out all the details required to keep a bird in the air."

He thanked me for the compliment, then commended my willingness to repeatedly repair the broken bones of old "9-Lives" and for the way I could miraculously get it back into flying order. He said, "I don't think I have the patience you have to put one together!"

That evening, I made a deal with Nathan that gave birth
to a saying between us that we have used a number of times
since. I said, "Nate, I'll build 'em; you fly 'em!" He agreed
. . . and it remained that way. We discovered that we were a
team. Where I was weak, he was strong. Where he faltered, I
picked up the load. Through the trips to that church parking
lot with our multi-mended model, my son got an up-close
view of the importance of working together. He recognized
that in his years ahead, sometimes he would need to join
hands with someone else in order to get a job done. He was
able to see clearly that very often, teamwork is the key to
success. The virtues of accepting the talents of others, and
being willing to combine strengths serve a man well.

Not too long ago, that saying born out of our time with
old "9-Lives" cropped up again. In our studio, in the middle
of a session with a high-dollar fiddle player doing over-dubs
on one of our songs, one of the recording machines decided
to break down. The tape jammed and would not eject. We
had a back-up copy but it was worthless if the machine
would not let go of the damaged tape. Nathan was producing the session when the problem arose, and he was at a
complete loss about how to remedy it. The fiddle player
took a break and called one of his friends who was a techni-
cian, but he hit a dead end. Nathan called the manufactur-
ers. As he tried to explain our emergency to them, I decided
to take the machine apart and look inside. I found that the
pinch-rollers had "eaten" the tape and turned it into an
ugly, tangled, dangerously wrinkled mess. It was costing us
money since the player was working by the hour, so I started
to fiddle with the machine and see if I could come up with a

fix. I traced the tape path and found a little white plastic rod that spun between my fingers. When I turned it, I the tape cartridge began to release from the machine, and I manually removed the tape. Within a few minutes, after cleaning the pinch rollers and other vital parts, we inserted the back-up. Our guest musician took his place back at the microphone and re-tuned his instrument, Nathan and I looked at each other in relief. That's when I said to my young producer, "I'll build 'em; you fly 'em!" We high-fived as he smiled in agreement and then carefully pushed the play/record buttons and we went about our business of over-dubs. Once again, teamwork had paid off.

It's been a long time since Nathan and I have heard the ear-piercing buzz of that old wooden model. I miss it. From time to time, I toy with the idea of buying a new kit and trying my hand at flying again. However, to do so would seem almost disrespectful to old "9-Lives." He waits for us in the attic. He's up there somewhere, buried with all the other evidence of our toy-hood. It may be scarred, battered and ugly, but it will always be a precious treasure to us because it always reminds us of a time we had together . . . outside . . . as a team!

16

Mom Gets the Last Word

Steve and the children have never had any problem with finding fun tucked away in whatever job is put before them. (The yard-work project is a perfect example of their turning work into play.) Having been raised on a dairy farm and being one of six children, however, I have always found more opportunities, as well as a need, to work than to play. Recreation has never come easily to me.

Since my family has found the great outdoors to be such an enjoyable part of their lives, they have often encouraged me to explore the wonderful world that awaits us in nature. In my book, *Running on Empty (And Looking for the Nearest Exit)*, I tell about one of the few times I gave in to their prodding and went outside to play.

> *"Let's take a vacation day and go fishing," my family urged. "You need it, Mom. You need to get away from everything and enjoy the great outdoors."*
>
> *A perfect opportunity was coming up. The four of us were scheduled to sing in Alaska. So we made plans to stay over an extra day—for fun, rest and adventure. Since I had never gone on any of the Famous Family Fishing Forays before, I resisted my regular tendency to be a stick-in-the-mud. I decided to trust my family to*

spirit me away in a small plane into the bush country of Alaska for a day of fishing. We were going to fish for King Salmon. It would be fun!

The basic reason I've never accompanied my family on fishing trips: I don't like to fish. I don't like the smell or the feel of fish. And unless they're heavily battered and deep-fried, I don't even like the taste of fish. And I'm not that crazy about the great outdoors, unless I'm poolside in a lounge chair with my tanning oils and a cold drink. Braving the elements and battling the wild did not sound that appealing, but being the dutiful mother, I cheerfully went along. So I could relax.

The morning started rather early with the buzz of the clock radio. Getting up at 5 A.M. so we could relax seemed a bit strange to me, but who was I to complain? We gathered the gear, the ice cooler, and the waders. (Waders are hip boots you wear so you won't get wet while standing in the middle of a rushing river.) Soon our family sardine-squeezed into the little float-plane, along with three other men and their gear. I could begin to see the wild horizon of rugged mountains now in the blue light of dawn. But I had no idea what public humiliation loomed just beyond them.

The first glitch came when the pilot noticed the pontoons were sitting a bit low in the water. The total weight of the plane concerned him. He stuck his head into the passenger compartment and there—in front of every-one—asked us to tell our weight...Out loud! You must understand, I don't tell anyone what I weigh. My husband of nearly a quarter of a century—the father of my children, my soulmate—does not know what the scales and I know.

Everything seemed to shift into slow motion. The plane got deathly silent, and all eyes turned accusingly on me, as if to say, "If you lie and this plane goes down, it will be all your fault." In my mind's eye I could see the headlines in the tabloids: WOMAN LIES ABOUT HER WEIGHT, KILLING ENTIRE FAMILY. Life and death had me by the throat. I took a deep breath, and before God and the angels I said. "_____." (Are you kidding? Did you really think I'd tell you, too?)

Everyone seemed unusually quiet. I just knew someone was thinking, "Lady, that's what my car weighs . . ."

Heidi, our daughter, was stunned. In an ominous whisper, she said, "You told your weight?!" I gave no reply. I was already tired and miserable.

As I stared out the window moments later, deafened by the propellers' roar, I suspected my chances of feeling refreshed and relaxed were slim. And that was the only thing that was slim that day.

It got worse when we pontooned to a landing on a wilderness river and I realized the pilot was leaving us in the bush country. Oh sure, he said he'd return that evening at six o'clock. But did anyone really know this man? All that was left for me was to resign myself to enjoy fishing . . . for the next ten hours!

We made our way to the site where the fish were supposed to be. It was quite exhilarating: the breathtaking scenery, the bitter cold wind, and the bloodsucking mosquitoes. Since I had never fished, I was instructed in how to cast the line into the water and found, to my amazement, that it wasn't so bad after all.

Heidi is quite an enthusiastic fisherman. It's fun to see her standing beside her dad, fishing with true enjoyment. About forty-five minutes into that morning's sport, Heidi decided to move off the sandbar where we were fishing and go to the other side. When she changed positions, she accidentally stepped off the sandbar and up to her waist in water, well over her waders. She was soaked. The air was around fifty degrees, and the water was much colder.

Here we were, stranded in the middle of nowhere, and I had not thought to bring a stitch of extra clothing. No towels or blankets. We fished Heidi from the river, and fortunately, one of the men who was fishing alongside us let Heidi change into the extra clothes he'd brought. We made a fire and warmed Heidi up, and soon the problem was solved so everyone could get back to fishing . . . everyone, that is, except me. As the family enjoyed an invigorating morning on the river, the "eternal mother" stood on the shore like a human clothesline, continuously turning Heidi's clothes, drying them by the fire. Wasn't this fun!

Every once in a while someone would call back to me from his fishing spot and ask, "How's it going? Are you all right?" Heidi yelled over, "Don't burn my jeans, Mom! Those are my favorites."

Yes, my family was right. I needed a day away from the mundane routine of everyday chores—you know, like doing laundry. Standing there on the shore trying to keep from singeing Heidi's jeans and unsuccessfully *keeping smoke out of my eyes, I gained a newfound appreciation for my life. There was even a special spot of affection for my electric clothes dryer.*

With Heidi's clothes finally dried, I returned to the river—smelling like a hot dog. The rest of the day was great fun and very relaxing. I definitely want to go fishing again . . . someday . . . maybe . . . (if my family grovels). . . .

Even though I have on occasion succumbed to the lure of the outdoors, I have found my most profound contribution to my family's love of adventure is basically "staying out of the way." I am very grateful that Steve sincerely desired to teach our children how to function and enjoy being outside because it has yielded a valuable bond between a father and his kids. In the closing verse of the Old Testament we are told that in the last days God will "restore the hearts of the fathers to their children, and the hearts of the children to their fathers, lest I come and smite the land with a curse" (Malachi 4:6). Our land is indeed "cursed" because too many fathers have not been a part of their children's lives. It takes an enormous amount of time and effort on the part of a dad to cultivate this love relationship. And in our family, the outdoors has been the most conducive setting for this closeness to grow.

While I readily admit that I am genuinely afraid that something will happen in the woods, along the river, in the boat, or even on the golf course (have you ever seen Steve play golf?), I have learned to put my entire family in the hands of God, and to trust Him for their safety. I humbly acknowledge that any risk is well worth the result of Steve and the children's hearts being strengthened and restored. Also, it is a comfort to know that the character building lessons which Nathan and Heidi bring in from the great outdoors will go with them all of their lives.

I would also add, in most recent years my family has graciously accepted the fact that I may not want to participate in all the activities they find enjoyable. There is always a standing invitation to go along, and sometimes I do. However, I appreciate that my special interest, the flower garden, is not only encouraged, but applauded. When Steve and the kids come home after spending a long day in a canoe or on a bicycle, we can all retire to the patio and drink our tea; they can tell their wild exploits, and we enjoy a sit among the vivid colors of my beautiful flowers. What a wonderful blessing just to be together . . . outside!

About the Author

Proudly claiming West Virginia as his home state, Steve Chapman grew up as the son of a preacher. He met his wife, Annie, in junior high school in 1963. In March of 1975, they married after dating a few months and settled in Nashville, Tennessee. There they have raised their son and daughter, Nathan and Heidi.

Steve is president of S&A Family, Inc., an organization formed to oversee the production of the Chapmans' recorded music. They have had "family life" as the theme of their lyrics since they began singing together in 1980. As Dove Award-winning artists, their schedule sends them to over 100 cities a year to present concerts that feature songs from over 15 recorded projects.

Steve's love of hunting began in his early teens on a weekend when one of his dad's church members invited him to tag along on an October squirrel hunt. Archery is his first choice for use in the field, followed by muzzle loader, and then pistol or rifle. To date, according to Steve's calculations, he has entered the woods before daylight on at least a thousand mornings. He says he hopes for just as many more.

Recordings

The song lyrics found in these pages are from the following recorded projects:

"Man to Man"
From Tools for the Trade/Steve and Annie Chapman
S&A Family, Inc., Cassette SA-7000/CD SACD-7000

"The Arrow and the Bow"
From Guest of Honor/Steve and Annie Chapman/Star
Song Communications

"Seasons of a Man"
From Tools for the Trade/Steve & Annie Chapman
S&A Family, Inc., Cassette SA-7000/CD SACD-7000

"Reachable"
From Reachable/Steve and Annie Chapman/
S&A Family, Inc.
Cassette SA-6000/CD SACD-6000

"The Key"
From Reachable/Steve and Annie Chapman/
S&A Family, Inc.,
Cassette SA-6000/CD SACD-6000

For a list of available products
(CD's/cassettes/videos/books)
or more information about the Chapmans
please write to:

S&A Family, Inc.
P.O. Box 535
Madison, TN 37116